WITHDRAWN

Modern Critical Interpretations
# Arthur Miller's
# All My Sons

# Modern Critical Interpretations

*These and other titles in preparation*

*Modern Critical Interpretations*

# Arthur Miller's
# All My Sons

*Edited and with an introduction by*
Harold Bloom
*Sterling Professor of the Humanities*
*Yale University*

*Chelsea House Publishers* ◊ *1988*

NEW YORK ◊ NEW HAVEN ◊ PHILADELPHIA

Printed and bound in the United States of America

10   9   8   7   6   5   4   3   2   1

∞ The paper used in this publication meets the minimum
requirements of the American National Standard for
Permanence of Paper for Printed Library Materials,
Z39.48-1984.

Library of Congress Cataloging-in-Publication Data
Arthur Miller's All my sons.
    (Modern critical interpretations)
    Bibliography: p.
    Includes index.
    Summary: A collection of critical essays on Miller's drama
"All my sons" arranged in chronological order of publication.
    1. Miller, Arthur, 1915–    . All my sons.    [1. Miller,
Arthur, 1915–    . All my sons. 2. American literature—
History and criticism]    I. Bloom, Harold.   II. Series.
PS3525.I5156A7335   1988        812'.52        87–27744
ISBN 1–55546–060–7 (alk. paper)

# Contents

# Editor's Note

This book brings together a representative selection of the best critical interpretations devoted to Arthur Miller's drama *All My Sons*. The critical essays are reprinted here in the chronological order of their original publication. I am grateful to Daniel Duffy and Henry Finder for their assistance in editing this volume.

My introduction seeks to define how *All My Sons* achieves aesthetic dignity despite Miller's limitations, at that point, as a dramatic writer. Arthur Miller himself follows with his own statement as to his intentions: "The structure of the play is designed to bring a man into the direct path of the consequences he has wrought."

The director Harold Clurman praises *All My Sons,* even though it lacks poetic vision, because of the passionate persistence of Miller's moral talent. In the reading of Samuel A. Yorks, the play is divided between Miller's intellect, speaking through Chris Keller, and Miller's emotions, clinging to Joe and Kate Keller. Arvin R. Wells reflects upon the same division, arguing that the drama's action stresses moral responsibility while showing also the inadequacy of a rigid idealism, as incarnated in Chris.

The influence of Ibsen upon *All My Sons* is traced by Sheila Huftel, who finds the theme of evasion to be dominant both in Miller's play and in Miller's adaption of Ibsen's *An Enemy of the People*. Edward Murray finds in *All My Sons* a failure to apprehend the complexity of human experience, while Barry Gross indicts the play for failing to understand the larger moral context that it necessarily invokes.

In Orm Överland's analysis, Miller is valuable only when he works in the forms of realism and is uneasy when he departs from realistic conventions. Dennis Welland regards *All My Sons* as a social study of the bewilderments of a common man who cannot learn moral responsibilities to others. This is akin to the emphasis of Leonard Moss, who finds in the play a successful social perspective but a relative failure in language.

C. W. E. Bigsby finds in *All My Sons* an Ibsenite well-made play, but not yet the true, direct engagement that Miller will manifest, in later plays, with the dreams and anxieties of the American people. The dramatic strategy of the play, as expounded by June Schlueter, is a web or network of faith and belief that snaps under pressure. Steven R. Centola concludes this volume with a previously unpublished essay that sees *All My Sons* as a deep study in bad faith, defined as the denial of freedom and responsibility in each individual, when that individual himself is the denier.

# Introduction

## I

Rather like Eugene O'Neill before him, Arthur Miller raises, at least for me, the difficult critical question as to whether there is not an element in drama that is other than literary, even contrary in value (supposed or real) to literary values, perhaps even to aesthetic values. O'Neill, a very nearly great dramatist, particularly in *The Iceman Cometh* and *Long Day's Journey into Night,* is not a good writer, except perhaps in his stage directions. Miller is by no means a bad writer, but he is scarcely an eloquent master of the language. I have just reread *All My Sons, Death of a Salesman,* and *The Crucible,* and am compelled to reflect how poorly they reread, though all of them, properly staged, are very effective dramas, and *Death of a Salesman* is considerably more than that. It ranks with *Iceman, Long Day's Journey,* Williams's *A Streetcar Named Desire,* Wilder's *The Skin of Our Teeth* and Albee's *The Zoo Story* as one of the half-dozen crucial American plays. Yet its literary status seems to me somewhat questionable, which returns me to the issue of what there is in drama that can survive indifferent or even poor writing.

Defending *Death of a Salesman,* despite what he admits is a sentimental glibness in its prose, Kenneth Tynan memorably observed: "But the theater is an impure craft, and *Death of a Salesman* organizes its impurities with an emotional effect unrivalled in postwar drama." The observation still seems true, a quarter-century after Tynan made it, yet how unlikely a similar statement would seem if ventured about Ibsen, Miller's prime precursor. Do we speak of *Hedda Gabler* organizing its impurities with an unrivalled emotional effect? Why is the American drama, except for Thornton Wilder (its one great sport), addicted to an organization of impurities, a critical phrase perhaps applicable only to Theodore Dreiser, among the major American novelists? Why is it that we have brought forth *The Scarlet Letter, Moby-Dick, Adventures of Huckleberry Finn, The Portrait of a Lady, The Sun*

1

*Also Rises, The Great Gatsby, As I Lay Dying, Miss Lonelyhearts, The Crying of Lot 49,* but no comparable dramas? How can a nation whose poets include Whitman, Dickinson, Frost, Stevens, Eliot, Hart Crane, Elizabeth Bishop, James Merrill, and John Ashbery, among so many others of the highest aesthetic dignity—how can it offer us only O'Neill, Miller, and Williams as its strongest playwrights?

Drama at its most eminent tends not to appear either too early or too late in any national literature. The United States may be the great exception, since before O'Neill we had little better than Clyde Fitch, and our major dramas (it is to be hoped) have not yet manifested themselves. I have seen little speculation upon this matter, with the grand exception of Alvin B. Kernan, the magisterial scholarly critic of Shakespeare and of Elizabethan dramatic literature. Meditating upon American plays, in 1967, Kernan tuned his initially somber notes to hopeful ones:

> Thus with all our efforts, money, and good intentions, we have not yet achieved a theater; and we have not, I believe, because we do not see life in historic and dramatic terms. Even our greatest novelists and poets, sensitive and subtle though they are, do not think dramatically, and should not be asked to, for they express themselves and us in other forms more suited to their visions (and ours). But we have come very close at moments to having great plays, if not a great theatrical tradition. When the Tyrone family stands in its parlor looking at the mad mother holding her wedding dress and knowing that all the good will in the world cannot undo what the past has done to them; when Willy Loman, the salesman, plunges again and again into the past to search for the point where it all went irremediably wrong and cannot find any one fatal turning point; when the Antrobus family, to end on a more cheerful note, drafts stage hands from backstage to take the place of sick actors, gathers its feeble and ever-disappointed hopes, puts its miserable home together again after another in a series of unending disasters stretching from the ice age to the present; then we are very close to accepting our entanglement in the historical process and our status as actors, which may in time produce a true theater.

That time has not yet come, twenty years later, but I think that Kernan was more right even than he knew. Our greatest novelists and poets continue not to see life in historic and dramatic terms, precisely because our literary tradition remains incurably Emersonian, and Emerson shrewdly dismissed both history and drama as European rather than American. An overtly anti-Emersonian poet-novelist like Robert Penn Warren does see life in historic and dramatic terms, and yet has done his best work away from the stage, despite his effort to write *All the King's Men* as a play. Our foremost novelist, Henry James, failed as a dramatist, precisely because he was more Emersonian than he knew, and turned too far inward in nuanced vision for a play to be his proper mode of representation. One hardly sees Faulkner or Frost, Hemingway or Stevens as dramatists, though they all made their attempts. Nor would a comparison of *The Waste Land* and *The Family Reunion* be kind to Eliot's dramatic ambitions. The American literary mode, whether narrative or lyric, tends towards romance and rumination, or fantastic vision, rather than drama. Emerson, genius of the shores of America, directed us away from history, and distrusted drama as a revel. Nothing is got for nothing; Faulkner and Wallace Stevens, aesthetic light-years beyond O'Neill and Tennessee Williams, seem to mark the limits of the literary imagination in our American century. It is unfair to *All My Sons* and *Death of a Salesman* to read them with the high expectations we rightly bring to *As I Lay Dying* and *Notes toward a Supreme Fiction*. Miller, a social dramatist, keenly aware of history, fills an authentic American need, certainly for his own time.

## II

*All My Sons* (1947), Miller's first success, retains the flavor of post-World War II America, though it is indubitably something beyond a period piece. Perhaps all of Miller's work could be titled *The Guilt of the Fathers,* which is a dark matter for a Jewish playwright, brought up to believe in the normative tradition, with its emphasis upon the virtues of the fathers. Though it is a truism to note that *All My Sons* is an Ibsenite play, the influence relation to Ibsen remains authentic, and is part of the play's meaning, in the sense that Ibsen too is one of the fathers, and shares in their guilt. Ibsen's peculiar guilt in *All My Sons* is to have appropriated most of Miller's available stock of dramatic language. The result is that this drama is admirably constructed yet not adequately expressed. It is not just that eloquence is lacking; sometimes the characters seem unable to say what they need to say if we are to be with them as we should.

Joe Keller ought to be the hero-villain of *All My Sons,* since pragmatically he certainly is a villain. But Miller is enormously fond of Joe, and so are we; he is not a good man, and yet he lives like one, in regard to family, friends, neighbors. I do not think that Miller ever is interested in Hannah Arendt's curious notion of the banality of evil. Joe is banal, and he is not evil though his business has led him into what must be called moral idiocy, in regard to his partner and to any world that transcends his own immediate family. Poor Joe is just not very intelligent, and it is Miller's curious gift that he can render such a man dramatically interesting. An ordinary man who wants to have a moderately good time, who wants his family never to suffer, and who lacks any imagination beyond the immediate: what is this except an authentic American Everyman? The wretched Joe simply is someone who does not know enough, indeed who scarcely knows anything at all. Nor can he learn anything. What I find least convincing in the play is Joe's moment of breaking through to a moral awareness, and a new kind of knowledge:

> MOTHER: Why are you going? You'll sleep, why are you going?
> KELLER: I can't sleep here. I'll feel better if I go.
> MOTHER: You're so foolish. Larry was your son too, wasn't he? You know he'd never tell you to do this.
> KELLER (*looking at letter in his hand*): Then what is this if it isn't telling me? Sure, he was my son. But I think to him they were all my sons. And I guess they were, I guess they were. I'll be right down. *Exits into house.*
> MOTHER (*to Chris, with determination*): You're not going to take him!
> CHRIS: I'm taking him.
> MOTHER: It's up to you, if you tell him to stay he'll stay. Go and tell him!
> CHRIS: Nobody could stop him now.
> MOTHER: You'll stop him! How long will he live in prison? Are you trying to kill him?

Nothing in Joe is spiritually capable of seeing and saying: "They were all my sons. And I guess they were, I guess they were." That does not reverberate any more persuasively than Chris crying out: "There's a universe of people outside and you're responsible to it." Drama fails Miller there, or perhaps he fails drama. Joe Keller was too remote from a felt sense of reality for Miller to represent the estrangement properly, except in regard to the blindness Joe manifested towards his two sons. Miller crossed over into his one permanent achievement when he swerved from Ibsen into the marginal world of *Death of a Salesman,* where the pain is the meaning, and the meaning has a repressed but vital relationship to the normative vision that informs Jewish memory.

# The Question of Relatedness

*Arthur Miller*

When *All My Sons* opened on Broadway it was called an "Ibsenesque" play. Some people liked it for this reason and others did not. Ibsen is relevant to this play but what he means to me is not always what he means to others, either his advocates or his detractors. More often than not, these days, he is thought of as a stage carpenter with a flair for ideas of importance. The whole aim of shaping a dramatic work on strict lines which will elicit a distinct meaning reducible to a sentence is now suspect. "Life" is now more complicated than such a mechanical contrasting of forces can hope to reflect. Instead, the aim is a "poetic" drama, preferably one whose ultimate thought or meaning is elusive, a drama which appears not to have been composed or constructed, but which somehow comes to life on a stage and then flickers away. To come quickly to the point, our theater inclines toward the forms of adolescence rather than analytical adulthood. It is not my place to deal in praise or blame but it seems to me that a fair judge would be compelled to conclude, as a minimum, that the run of serious works of the past decade have been written and played under an intellectually—as well as electrically—diffused light. It is believed that any attempt to "prove" something in a play is somehow unfair and certainly inartistic, if not gauche, more particularly if what is being proved happens to be in any overt way of social moment. Indeed, one American critic believes that the narrowness of the theater audience—as compared with that for movies and television— is the result of the masses' having been driven away from the theater by plays that preached.

5

This is not, of course, a new attitude in the world. Every major playwright has had to make his way against it, for there is and always will be a certain amount of resentfulness toward the presumption of any playwright to teach. And there will never be a satisfactory way of explaining that no playwright can be praised for his high seriousness and at the same time be praised for not trying to teach; the very conception of a dramatic theme inevitably means that certain aspects of life are selected and others left out, and to imagine that a play can be written disinterestedly is to believe that one can make love disinterestedly.

The debatable question is never whether a play ought to teach but whether it is art, and in this connection the basic criterion—purely technical considerations to one side—is the passion with which the teaching is made. I hasten to add the obvious—that a work cannot be judged by the validity of its teaching. But it is entirely misleading to state that there is some profound conflict between art and the philosophically or socially meaningful theme. I say this not out of a preference for plays that teach but in deference to the nature of the creative act. A work of art is not handed down from Olympus from a creature with a vision as wide as the world. If that could be done a play would never end, just as history has no end. A play must end, and end with a climax, and to forge a climax the forces in life, which are of infinite complexity, must be made finite and capable of a more or less succinct culmination. Thus, all dramas are to that extent arbitrary—in comparison with life itself—and embody a viewpoint if not an obsession on the author's part. So that when I am told that a play is beautiful and (or because) it does not try to teach anything, I can only wonder which of two things is true about it: either what it teaches is so obvious, so inconsiderable as to appear to the critic to be "natural," or its teaching has been embedded and articulated so thoroughly in the action itself as not to appear as an objective but only a subjective fact.

*All My Sons* was not my first play but the eighth or ninth I had written up to the mid-forties. But for the one immediately preceding it, none of the others were produced in the professional theater, and since the reader can have little knowledge of this one—which lasted less than a week on Broadway—and no knowledge at all of the others, a word is in order about these desk-drawer plays, particularly the failure called *The Man Who Had All the Luck*.

This play was an investigation to discover what exact part a man played in his own fate. It deals with a young man in a small town who, by the time he is in his mid-twenties, owns several growing businesses, has married the girl he loves, is the father of a child he has always wanted, and is daily becoming convinced that as his desires are gratified he is causing to accumulate around his own head an invisible but nearly palpable fund, so to speak, of retribution. The law of life, as he observes life around him, is that people are always frustrated in some important regard; and he conceives that he must be too, and the play is built around his conviction of impending disaster. The disaster never comes, even when, in effect, he tries to bring it on in order to survive it and find peace. Instead, he comes to believe in his own superiority, and in his remarkable ability to succeed.

Now, more than a decade later, it is possible for me to see that far from being a waste and a failure this play was a preparation, and possibly a necessary one, for those that followed, especially *All My Sons* and *Death of a Salesman,* and this for many reasons. In the more than half-dozen plays before it I had picked themes at random—which is to say that I had had no awareness of any inner continuity running from one of these plays to the next, and I did not perceive myself in what I had written. I had begun with a play about a family, then a play about two brothers caught on either side of radicalism in a university, then a play about a psychologist's dilemma in a prison where the sane were inexorably moving over to join the mad, a play about a bizarre ship's officer whose desire for death led him to piracy on the seas, a tragedy on the Cortes-Montezuma conflict, and others. Once again, as I worked on *The Man Who Had All the Luck* I was writing, I would have said, about what lay outside me. I had heard the story of a young man in a midwestern town who had earned the respect and love of his town and great personal prosperity as well, and who, suddenly and for no known reason, took to suspecting everyone of wanting to rob him, and within a year of his obsession's onset had taken his own life.

In the past I had rarely spent more than three months on a play. Now the months went by with the end never in sight. After nearly ten years of writing I had struck upon what seemed a bottomless pit of mutually canceling meanings and implications. In the past I had had less difficulty with forming a "story" and more with the exploration of its meanings. Now, in contrast, I was working with an overwhelming sense of meaning, but however I tried I could not make the drama continuous and of a piece; it persisted, with the beginning of each scene, in starting afresh as though each scene were the beginning of a new play. Then one day, while I was lying on a beach, a simple shift of relationships came to mind, a shift which did not and could not solve the problem of writing *The Man Who Had All the Luck,* but, I think now, made at least two of the plays that followed possible, and a great deal else besides.

What I saw, without laboring the details, was that two of the characters, who had been friends in the previous drafts, were logically brothers and had the same father. Had I known then what I know now I could have saved myself a lot of trouble. The play was impossible to fix because the overt story was only tangential to the secret drama its author was quite unconsciously trying to write. But in writing of the father-son relationship and of the son's search for his relatedness there was a fullness of feeling I had never known before; a crescendo was struck with a force I could almost touch. The crux of *All My Sons,* which would not be written until nearly three years later, was formed; and the roots of *Death of a Salesman* were sprouted.

The form of *All My Sons* is a reflection and an expression of several forces, of only some of which I was conscious. I desired above all to write rationally, to write so that I could tell the story of the play to even an unlettered person and spark a look of recognition on his face. The accusation I harbored against the earlier play was that it could not make sense to commonsense people. I have always been in love with wonder, the wonder of how things and people got to be what they are, and in *The Man Who Had All the Luck* I had tried to grasp wonder, I had tried to make it on the stage, by writing wonder. But wonder had betrayed me and the only other course I had was the one I took—to seek cause and effect, hard actions, facts, the geometry of relationships, and to hold back any tendency to express an idea in itself unless it was literally forced out of a character's mouth; in other words, to let wonder rise up like a mist, a gas, a vapor from the gradual and remorseless crush of factual and psychological conflict. I went back to the great book of wonder, *The Brothers Karamazov,* and I found what suddenly I felt must be true of it: that if one reads its most colorful, breathtaking, wonderful pages, one finds the thickest concentration of hard facts. Facts about the biographies of the characters, about the kind of bark on the moonlit trees, the way a window is hinged, the exact position of Dmitri as he peers through the window at his father, the precise description of his father's dress. Above all, the precise collision of inner themes during, not before or after, the high dramatic scenes. And quite as suddenly I noticed in Beethoven the holding back of climax until it was ready, the grasp of the rising line and the unwillingness to divert to an easy climax until the true one was ready. If there is one word to name the mood I felt it was *Forego.* Let nothing interfere with the shape, the direction, the intention. I believed that I had felt too much in the previous play and understood too little.

I was turning thirty then, the author of perhaps a dozen plays, none of which I could truly believe were finished. I had written many scenes, but not a play. A play, I saw then, was an organism of which I had fashioned only certain parts. The decision formed to write one more, and if again it turned out to be unrealizable, I would go into another line of work. I have never loved the brick and mortar of the theater, and only once in my life had I been truly engrossed in a production—when Ruth Gordon played in the Jed Harris production of *A Doll's House*. The sole sense of connection with theater came when I saw the productions of the Group Theatre. It was not only the brilliance of ensemble acting, which in my opinion has never been equaled since in America, but the air of union created between actors and the audience. Here was the promise of prophetic theater which suggested to my mind the Greek situation when religion and belief were the heart of drama. I watched the Group Theatre from fifty-five-cent seats in the balcony, and at intermission time it was possible to feel the heat and the passion of people moved not only in their bellies but in their thoughts. If I say that my own writer's ego found fault with the plays it does not detract from the fact that the performances were almost all inspiring to me, and when I heard that the Group was falling apart it seemed incredible that a society of saints—which they were to me, artistically, even as I had never met one of them—should be made up of people with less than absolute dedication to their cause.

*All My Sons* was begun several years after the Group had ceased to be, but it was what I can only call now a play written for a prophetic theater. I am aware of the vagueness of the term but I cannot do very well at defining what I mean. Perhaps it signifies a theater, a play, which is meant to become part of the lives of its audience—a play seriously meant for people of common sense, and relevant to both their domestic lives and their daily work, but an experience which widens their awareness of connection—the filaments to the past and the future which lie concealed in "life."

My intention in this play was to be as untheatrical as possible. To that end any metaphor, any image, any figure of speech, however creditable to me, was removed if it even slightly brought to consciousness the hand of a writer. So far as was possible nothing was to be permitted to interfere with its artlessness.

It seems to me now that I had the attitude of one laying siege to a fortress in this form. The sapping operation was to take place without a sound beneath a clear landscape in the broad light of a peaceful day. Nor was this approach arbitrary. It grew out of a determination to reverse my past playwriting errors, and from the kind of story I happened to have discovered.

During an idle chat in my living room, a pious lady from the Middle

West told of a family in her neighborhood which had been destroyed when the daughter turned the father in to the authorities on discovering that he had been selling faulty machinery to the army. The war was then in full blast. By the time she had finished the tale I had transformed the daughter into a son and the climax of the second act was full and clear in my mind.

I knew my informant's neighborhood, I knew its middle-class ordinariness, and I knew how rarely the great issues penetrate such environments. But the fact that a girl had not only wanted to, but had actually moved against an erring father transformed into fact and common reality what in my previous play I had only begun to hint at. I had no awareness of the slightest connection between the two plays. All I knew was that somehow a hard thing had entered into me, a crux toward which it seemed possible to move in strong and straight lines. Something was crystal clear to me for the first time since I had begun to write plays, and it was the crisis of the second act, the revelation of the full loathesomeness of an antisocial action.

With this sense of dealing with an existing objective fact, I began to feel a difference in my role as a writer. It occurred to me that I must write this play so that even the actual criminal, on reading it, would have to say that it was true and sensible and as real as his life. It began to seem to me that what I had written until then, as well as almost all the plays I had ever seen, had been written for a theatrical performance, when they should have been written as a kind of testimony whose relevance far surpassed theatrics.

For these reasons the play begins in an atmosphere of undisturbed normality. Its first act was later called slow, but it was designed to be slow. It was made so that even boredom might threaten, so that when the first intimation of the crime is dropped a genuine horror might begin to move into the heart of the audience, a horror born of the contrast between the placidity of the civilization on view and the threat to it that a rage of conscience could create.

It took some two years to fashion this play, chiefly, I think now, because of a difficulty not unconnected with a similar one in the previous play. It was the question of relatedness. The crime in *All My Sons* is not one that is about to be committed but one that has long since been committed. There is no question of its consequences' being ameliorated by anything Chris Keller or his father can do; the damage has been done irreparably. The stakes remaining are purely the conscience of Joe Keller and its awakening to the evil he has done, and the conscience of his son in the face of what he has discovered about his father. One could say that the problem was to make a fact of morality, but it is more precise, I think, to say that the structure of the play is designed to bring a man into the direct path of the consequences he has wrought. In one sense, it was the same problem of writing about David Beeves in the earlier play, for he too could not relate himself to what he had done. In both plays the dramatic obsession, so to speak, was with the twofold nature of the individual—his own concept of his deeds, and what turns out to be the "real" description of them. *All My Sons* has often been called a moral play, and it is that, but the concept of morality is not quite as purely ethical as it has been made to appear, nor is it so in the plays that follow. That the deed of Joe Keller at issue in *All My Sons* is his having been the cause of the death of pilots in war obscures the other kind of morality in which the play is primarily interested. Morality is probably a faulty word to use in the connection, but what I was after was the wonder in the fact that consequences of actions are as real as the actions themselves, yet we rarely take them into consideration as we perform actions, and we cannot hope to do so fully when we must always act with only partial knowledge of consequences. Joe Keller's trouble, in a word, is not that he cannot tell right from wrong but that his cast of mind cannot admit that he, personally, has any viable connection with his world, his universe, or his society. He is not a partner in society, but an incorporated member, so to speak, and you cannot sue personally the officers of a corporation. I hasten to make clear here that I am not merely speaking of a literal corporation but the concept of a man's becoming a function of production or distribution to the point where his personality becomes divorced from the actions it propels.

The fortress which *All My Sons* lays siege to is the fortress of unrelatedness. It is an assertion not so much of a morality in terms of right and wrong, but of a moral world's being such because men cannot walk away from certain of their deeds. In this sense Joe Keller is a threat to society and in this sense the play is a social play. Its "socialness" does not reside in its having dealt with the crime of selling defective materials to a nation at war—the same crime could easily be the basis of a thriller which would have no place in social dramaturgy. It is that the crime is seen as having roots in a certain relationship of the individual to society, and to a certain indoctrination he embodies, which, if dominant, can mean a jungle existence for all of us no matter how high our buildings soar. And it is in this sense that loneliness is socially meaningful in these plays.

To return to Ibsen's influence upon this play, I should have to split the question in order to make sense of it. First, there was the real impact of his work upon me at the time: this consisted mainly in what I then saw as his ability to forge a play upon a factual bedrock. A situation in his plays is never stated but revealed in terms of hard actions, irrevocable deeds; and sentiment is never confused with the action it conceals. Having for so long written in terms of what people felt rather than what they did, I turned to his works at the time with a sense of homecoming. As I have said, I wanted then to write so that people of common sense would mistake my play for life itself and not be required to lend it some poetic license before it could be believed. I wanted to make the moral world as real and evident as the immoral one so splendidly is.

But my own belief is that the shadow of Ibsen was seen on this play for another reason, and it is that *All My Sons* begins very late in its story. Thus, as in Ibsen's best-known work, a great amount of time is taken up with bringing the past into the present. In passing, I ought to add that this view of action is presently antipathetic to our commonly held feeling about the drama. More than any other quality of realism, or, to be more exact, of Ibsenism as a technique, this creates a sense of artificiality which we now tend to reject, for in other respects realism is still our reigning style. But it is no longer acceptable that characters should sit about discussing events of a year ago, or ten years ago, when in "life" they would be busy with the present. In truth, the effort to eliminate antecedent material has threatened to eliminate the past entirely from many plays. We are impatient to get on with it—so much so that anyone making a study of some highly creditable plays of the moment would be hard put to imagine what their characters were like a month before their actions and stories begin. *All My Sons* takes its time with the past, not in deference to Ibsen's method as I saw it then, but because its theme is the question of actions and consequences, and a way had to be found to throw a long line into the past in order to make that kind of connection viable.

That the idea of connection was central to me is indicated again in the kind of revision the play underwent. In its earlier versions the mother, Kate Keller, was in a dominating position; more precisely, her astrological beliefs were given great prominence. (The play's original title was *The Sign of the Archer*.) And this, because I sought in every sphere to give body and life to connection. But as the play progressed the conflict between Joe and his son Chris pressed astrology to the wall until its mysticism gave way to psychology. There was also the impulse to regard the mystical with suspicion, since it had, in the past, given me only turgid works that could never develop a true climax based upon revealed psychological truths. In short, where in previous plays I might well have been satisfied to create only an astrologically obsessed woman, the obsession now had to be opened up to reveal its core of self-interest and intention on the character's part. Wonder must have feet with which to walk the earth.

But before I leave this play it seems wise to say a few more words about the kind of dramatic impulse it represents, and one aspect of "Ibsenism" as a technique is the quickest path into that discussion. I have no vested interest in any one form—as the variety of forms I have used attests—but there is one element in Ibsen's method which I do not think ought to be overlooked, let alone dismissed as it so often is nowadays. If his plays, and his method, do nothing else they reveal the evolutionary quality of life. One is constantly aware, in watching his plays, of process, change, development. I think too many modern plays assume, so to speak, that their duty is merely to show the present countenance rather than to account for what happens. It is therefore wrong to imagine that because his first and sometimes his second acts devote so much time to a studied revelation of antecedent material, his view is static compared to our own. In truth, it is profoundly dynamic, for that enormous past was always heavily documented to the end that the present be comprehended with wholeness, as a moment in a flow of time, and not—as with so many modern plays—as a situation without roots. Indeed, even though I can myself reject other aspects of his work, it nevertheless presents barely and unadorned what I believe is the biggest single dramatic problem, namely, how to dramatize what has gone before. I say this not merely out of technical interest, but because dramatic characters, and the drama itself, can never hope to attain a maximum degree of consciousness unless they contain a viable unveiling of the contrast between past and present, and an awareness of the process by which the present has become what it is. And I say this, finally, because I take it as a truth that the end of drama is the creation of a higher consciousness and not merely a subjective attack upon the audience's nerves and feelings. What is precious in the Ibsen method is its insistence upon valid causation, and this cannot be dismissed as a wooden notion.

This is the "real" in Ibsen's realism for me, for he was, after all, as much a mystic as a realist. Which is simply to say that while there are mysteries in life which no amount of analyzing will reduce to reason, it is perfectly realistic to admit and even to proclaim that hiatus as a truth. But the problem is not to make complex what is essentially explainable; it is to make understandable what is complex without distorting and oversimplifying what cannot be explained. I think many of his devices are, in fact, quite arbitrary; that he betrays a Germanic ponderousness at times and a tendency to overprove what is quite clear in the first place. But we could do with more of his basic intention, which was to assert nothing he had not proved, and to cling always to the marvelous spectacle of life forcing one event out of the jaws of the preceding one and to reveal its elemental consistencies with surprise. In other words, I contrast his realism not with the lyrical, which I prize, but with sentimentality, which is always a leak in the dramatic dike. He sought to make a play as weighty and living a fact as the discovery of the steam engine or algebra. This can be scoffed away only at a price, and the price is a living drama.

# Thesis and Drama

## Harold Clurman

A dramatic critic eminent among dramatic critics recently wrote an article which suggested that plays "about something" were generally duds. The article was either very sly or very stupid. It was very sly insofar as it is unarguable that most plays the premise and sentiment of which we do not accept cannot please us. What was stupid in the article was to isolate "plays about something" into a special category of plays that are topical, political or, in some over-all manner, propaganda. Propaganda in the theatre may be defined as the other fellow's point of view or any position with which we disagree.

All plays are about something, whether or not they have an explicit thesis. *Peter Pan* is as much about something as *Candida*. *Cyrano de Bergerac* is as clear an expression of something as *Bury the Dead*. *The Iceman Cometh* is as much "propaganda" as *Deep Are the Roots*. *St. Joan* is as definitely a preachment as any play ever presented on Fourteenth Street by the old Theatre Union.

The critic's first job is to make clear what a play is about. Many reviewers are signally inept in the performance of this simple duty. The reason for this is that they mistake a play's materials for its meaning. It is as if an art critic were to say that Cézanne's painting is about apples, or to suppose that because religious subjects were used in many classic paintings all these paintings were necessarily inspired by religious feeling.

An artist generally finds it convenient to use the material he finds closest

From *Lies Like Truth: Theatre Reviews and Essays*. © 1947 by Harold Clurman. Macmillan, 1958.

at hand. What he says with his material always reveals something personal and distinct that cannot be described comprehensively merely by stating the materials he has employed. One play about a strike may convey some intimate frustration, another may be a lyric outburst of youthful aspiration. A slight comedy like Noel Coward's *Present Laughter* is not so much a play about the affairs of a successful playwright as a demonstration of a state of mind in which contempt and indifference to the world have been accepted as a sort of aristocratic privilege.

In the Simonov comedy *The Whole World Over,* which I directed, the subjects of the housing shortage and the rehabilitation of the veteran are brought into play, but they are not at all the essence of the matter. This comedy is essentially an image of faith and joy in everyday living, told in the folk tradition of those gay and sentimental songs which establish the continuity between what is universal in the spirit of the old and the new Russia.

Another play that has been variously characterized as a war play or as a play about the returned GI or as an attack on war profiteers is Arthur Miller's *All My Sons.* The central character of *All My Sons* is a small businessman who during the war sent out defective airplane parts which he hoped would not be used in actual combat but which he would not recall for fear his army contracts would be canceled and his business and his family ruined as a result. The play presents the gradual disclosure of these facts to the businessman's younger son, a former army officer. The revelation brings with it not only a realization that twenty-one boys were killed as a consequence of the use of the defective material but that the manufacturer's older son—an army pilot—committed suicide because of his father's crime. The younger son tries to make his father and mother understand that nothing—not business necessity nor devotion to family—can mitigate the father's guilt. A man must be responsible not alone to his wife and children but, ultimately, to all men. Failure to act on this fundamental tenet must inevitably lead to crime.

Contrary to what some reviewers have suggested, the author does not exonerate the central character by making the "system" responsible for his guilt. Such an explanation is the cogent but desperate excuse that the guilty man offers, but his son (and the author) emphatically deny his right to use it. There can be no evasion of the burden of individual human responsibility.

The distorted "individualism" of our day that makes the private good of the individual the final criterion for human action is shown to be inhuman and destructive, whereas the true individualism of our early American prophets made the individual responsible to the community. The man who blames society for his betrayal of it is a weakling and a coward. The individual of Arthur Miller's ethic is the guarantor in his own person of society's health. The difference between Arthur Miller's individualist and the believer in "rugged individualism" today is that the latter narrows his sense of self so that it extends no further than the family circle, while the former gives himself the scope of humanity.

What makes the theme of All My Sons increasingly important is that we constantly talk of "service" and repeat other residual phrases from the religions we inherit while we actually live a daily life devoted to the pursuit of Power or Success, the most unquestioned symbol of which is money. The real war in modern life is between a memory of morality and the pressure of "practicality." We live in a schizoid society. This is an open secret, but everybody pretends not to see it or condemns as "idealism" any attempt to remedy the condition. To understand that our double standard is a fatal disease is, as a matter of fact, the first step in a realistic attitude toward life. We shall see—at a later point of the present article—that it is this realism which a part of our society at the moment wishes to resist.

Some reviewers complain that the plot of All My Sons is too complicated. For a while I failed to understand what was meant by this criticism. Then I realized that the whole aspect of the mother's insistence that her son, reported missing, is alive—her clinging to every prop of belief, including the solace of astrological assurance—was what struck some of the reviewers as irrelevant. This is a misunderstanding that derives from thinking of the play as an exposé of war profiteering.

The war-profiteering aspect of the play, I repeat, represents the play's material, not its meaning. What Arthur Miller is dramatizing is a universal not a local situation. The mother, whose role in the explicit plot of the play is incidental, is the center of the play's meaning. She embodies the status quo or norm of our present-day ethic and behavior pattern. It is on her behalf that the husband has committed his crime. She, as well as what she represents, is his defense. But she cannot consciously accept the consequence of the morality she lives by, for in the end it is a morality that kills her children and even her husband. In order to retain her strength she cannot abandon her position—everything must be done for one's own—and yet it is this position that has destroyed what she hopes to protect. She is a "normal" woman, yet she is sick. She suffers from severe headaches; she is subject to anxiety dreams. She believes in the stars and with fervid complacency maintains that "some superstitions are very nice."

If there is a "villain" in the piece, it is the mother—the kindly, loving mother who wants her brood to be safe and her home undisturbed. When her husband, who believes too slavishly in her doctrine—it is the world's doctrine, and so there can be no fault with it—when her husband breaks down under the logic of her doctrine, which has made him a murderer, she has no better advice than, "Be smart!" Yet she, too, is innocent. When her son's friend, the doctor, mumbles: "How many people walking around loose, and they're crazy as coconuts. Money, money, money, money; you say it long enough, it doesn't mean anything. Oh how I'd love to be around when that happens," she answers, "You're so childish, Jim!" She is innocent because she cannot understand. Not even in the extremity of her grief does she understand. When her son tells her: "I'm like everybody else now. I'm practical now. You made me practical," she answers, "But you have to be." To her dying day, she will remain with this her only wisdom, her only conviction.

Her son cries out: "The cats in the alley are practical. The bums who ran away when we were fighting were practical. Only the dead ones weren't practical. But now I'm practical and I spit on myself. I'm going away." This is the essence of the playwright's meaning: "This is the land of the great big dogs. You don't love a man here, you eat him! That's the principle; the only one we live by . . . This is a zoo, a zoo!" The mother is sorry . . . deeply sorry. "What more can we be?" she asks. "You can be better!" her son answers, and it is the dramatist's answer as well.

Arthur Miller's talent is a moral talent with a passionate persistence that resembles that of the New England preacher who fashioned our first American rhetoric. *All My Sons* rouses and moves us even though it lacks the supreme fire of poetic vision. The determined thrust of its author's mind is not yet enough to melt or transfigure us, but in a theatre that has grown slothful it will have to do. Yes, it will do.

# Joe Keller and His Sons

*Samuel A. Yorks*

In his drama *All My Sons* Arthur Miller exploits a conflict of values that might have been a Greek theme. But for him this is more complex than for such a tragic author as Sophocles, who could in *Antigone,* for example, ground the clash between the moral law and the demands of the state in clearly defined religious and political practices. The moral law has in Miller's time lost much traditional force as the state has come to assert final authority even here. Security boards no more than Creon may respect the moral basis for individual action, and the abstractions of modern communication rule out that clarity of vision which allowed the Greeks to so forcefully present the basic issues. Joe Keller's is more cruel than Antigone's dilemma because it is not possible for him to see as clearly. The conflict that destroys him does not arise from the simple clash of Sophocles, but from society's own opposing commitments. His culture stresses the continuing right of the individual to economic aggrandizement while periodically calling for its nullification in the service of national abstractions, themselves a complex of humanity's universal aims and power politics.

Man's essential aloneness has created this vital problem because, isolated in mortal flesh, the individual attempts to somehow transcend the limitations of time and space. The ego seeks to lessen its anguish and finds in the clan and religion an extension of its being. Man's most acute sensibilities stem from this desire; for him the values of love and loyalty are supreme. For them he will kill or be killed. But tension that leads to ultimate

From *Western Humanities Review* 13, no. 4 (Autumn 1959). © 1959 by the University of Utah.

tragedy arises as individual aggressions become organized selfishness and the clan is transmuted into the state as man extends his biological and social affinities. The sphere of the individual is greatly enlarged in the process but extravagant payment may be demanded. Family security has become dependent upon the clan values, and in time of organized conflict these naturally become supreme. Ideally parallel, the demands of state and family then become antithetical and the individual may question his allegiance. He may be led to reject the rationalized slogans that accompany world power struggles or fail to understand the validity of the greater and more human ideals also embodied. If so, he may place his private loyalties first. This is the tragedy of Joe Keller; his society must understand rather than simply condemn him. He is a typical product of a century devoted to ideological power conflicts.

Miller presents the conflict of values in terms of a struggle between generations. The older Kellers fail to understand what the younger come to accept as the motive for the Second World War. Chris Keller reproaches his parents for their devotion to private and familial loyalties, for these are subordinate to the larger clan values he has found supreme among the men of his military unit who gave their lives for an ideal. Joe Keller cries that there is nothing bigger than the family; his son reminds him that he is responsible to a whole universe of people. Chris fails to distinguish whether his men were ultimately loyal to the announced ideal or to one another and so reproducing the more limited clan loyalty after all. Nor does Miller: his play never resolves its basic conflict. One feels that when Chris urges that as a result of the war sacrifices his people ought to be better in some way, he is speaking for the dramatist. But how "better" is no more clearly defined than the final loyalty of the men who died in battle. Presumably for Miller unit morale is related to the rightness of the cause, but some would question this in light of recent investigation. The frequent vagueness of crucial concepts may mirror the personal confusions of the writer torn by personal and ideological commitments in the war years and the play figure the symbolic gesture that betrays.

But *All My Sons* in its perverse and ambiguous affirmation of private loyalty is more than a revelation of personal conflicts, for it accurately foreshadowed Miller's subsequent stand before the congressional committee investigating alleged subversion. Those who fully realized the play's implications could have anticipated the outcome. Miller's resistance to the official inquisition was not based upon sympathy for leftist causes so much as upon his affirmation of the private person's dignity and rights. The playwright's blunt refusal to name certain individuals said to have been present at alleged Communist-inspired writers' conferences is parallel to the implied theme of this play. *All My Sons* actually affirms family loyalties, not those of the state.

Miller's idealistic stand and Joe Keller's seeming callous betrayal of the war effort seem antithetical. Had Joe been an idealist, would he not have been content to go down the financial drain to support the war effort? Superficially, at least, the tragedy indicates so and denies my argument, for the most obvious dramatized values seem clearly those affirming the one-worldism that was so potent in this country at the end of the Second World War. *All My Sons* appeared in 1947 at the height of this feeling in America, and it was at this time, too, that Miller's activities became what some politicians in retrospect deemed subversive. What makes this tragedy difficult of interpretation and seemingly irresolute is its mirroring of the writer's own conflicts during this period. As a record of a writer's experience this would not be unusual in the history of American letters. There is much evidence that art in America frequently arises from tensions generated by the opposed commitments of the artist. This is true of many European writers such as Balzac and Dostoevsky, who in their ambivalence alternately celebrated and excoriated Paris and God. But the principle, if it be one, is possibly uniquely true in the United States, because Americans have traditionally resisted and even denied irony in their cultural and esthetic attitudes. The recent glorification of irony and paradox by the critical formalists has possessed the ardor of the late converted. This absence of irony in traditional American writing has meant that artists seemed many times torn between options equally fervent and incompatible. *The Scarlet Letter* gained power because Hawthorne both supported and denied the Puritan doctrine; Melville in *Moby-Dick* argued for the comfort of the lee shore and for the necessary voyage; Stephen Crane was never finally certain whether Henry Fleming was caught in the moving box of necessity or had simply sinned; and Dreiser was both attracted and repelled as he peered with Sister Carrie into the store fronts of the rising tinsel city. An esthetic dialectic, largely unstated and even unconscious, exists in these typical works.

This rule seems true of Arthur Miller as well in *All My Sons*. Of course the obvious intention of the tragedy is to demonstrate that through his narrow and outdated loyalty to business and family—to the central image of the forty-foot front he feels bounds his world—Joe Keller betrayed the larger loyalties of the global conflict by shipping out defective engine parts for aircraft and killing many pilots, including his son Larry, who takes his life in shame. In his title Miller gives us to understand that Joe commits suicide because of his final recognition of all who fought as his sons. He had first thought to save his business and with it his boys' future by covering up his plant's error. After all, in our society a business to pass on to one's sons is a badge of honor for a life well spent. Joe obeys the values the clan has taught him. But it is also clear that Miller explicitly states he should have risked all for the larger dream by shouldering the blame instead of letting it fall upon his weaker and less guilty partner. This is clearly the conscious intent of the writer.

But is it not possible for other commitments to undercut this obvious theme? The dominance of the universal over the local loyalties is not unquestioned in this drama; Miller presents a case for more private values so strong that we are justified in sensing a strong bias to this view on his part. Because of this ambiguity, a certain dramatic confusion exists in Miller's play despite the clear intent. But this does not suggest merely artistic failure; it can imply an honest conflict of loyalties in one sensitive to contemporary stresses. Each must resolve as best he may these warring aims; possibly no easy resolution can be had by the thinking and feeling man today. Miller thought then he had solved the conflict by his sacrifice of local loyalty; a close examination of his drama may deny this.

## II

How does this opposition to the one-world view based upon abstract loyalty manifest itself within the play? Miller presents the strongest possible counterstatement. Joe Keller is above all loyal to his family—yet the dramatist presents him with insight and sympathy. Keller is consistently presented as "a man among men," and one capable of immense loyalty and affection. True, he is depicted as dodging responsibility at the time of the defective process in his plant by feigning illness and allowing his weaker partner to take the blame. But as he seeks to justify himself, Joe is allowed eloquence. He bitterly points out the profit motive that saturates the war effort: "Who worked for nothin' in that war? When they work for nothin', I'll work for nothin'. Did they ship a gun or a truck outa Detroit before they got their price? Is that clean? It's dollars and cents, nickels and dimes; war and peace, it's nickels and dimes, what's clean? Half the Goddamn country is gotta go if I go!" By his criticism of the national war effort Joe tries to obscure personal guilt but also points up the conflict of loyalties between the private clan and its extension, the state. Do all sacrifice equally for the total struggle or do some while others flourish? Is the abstract loyalty embodied in universal slogans really a monster feeding on the superior individual's finer sensibilities while pandering to the lusts of the callous and power oriented? Miller makes no obvious choice in *All My Sons* though he grants Joe Keller force and conviction. His cry lingers in our ears while we consider whether it is simple artistic integrity not to make of Joe a simple villain. Dramatic complexity is served in any event.

But the stature given Keller is only part of this contrary statement. What of mother Keller? Kate is easily the strongest individual in the play. She is shown as superior in force of character to all the others, especially in times of emotional crisis, except possibly when Anne presents for the first [time] Larry's letter. Kate affirms the most personal and private of loyalties; even when the letter destroys the family illusions her concern is for Joe rather than for herself. Mother Keller has dominated her husband by her knowledge of his actual guilt, but she subdues the hostile George Deever not by force but by the warmth of her response: "You offered it to him! *Give* it to him!" she exclaims to Anne Deever when she brings the grape juice to her brother. Kate Keller has for years protected her husband in crucial situations and has mastered others as well by her refusal to meet people on any level but that of the most direct, honest and personal. It is she who kept alive the myth that the lost son Larry would return. She does this to screen Joe, for if Larry is dead, then Joe killed him. This is not literally so, but in her mind Mrs. Keller connects Joe's guilty act with the absence of their son. And logic does not determine her thought; she is a creature of great emotion. Significantly, the most forceful and moving criticism of the war and its ideals is made by her as she rebuts the official views expressed by the rather sanctimonious Chris Keller. Referring to the pretty Lydia who married the zany Frank Lubey, mother Keller tells George Deever, "While you were getting mad about Fascism, Frank was getting into her bed." She also blasts the lofty ideals of the Eagle Scouts, as she terms George and her sons: "So now I got a tree." In addition to Larry's memorial, she laments Chris's bad feet and the aging George. One might again argue that this only demonstrates Miller's artistic control, for this woman's strong statement of a misguided personal loyalty only points the more vigorously to the intensity and complexity of the struggle between opposed ideals. But possibly this strongly emotional language echoes what is close to its creator's heart. What adds potency to Kate's attack upon the ideals of embattled democracy is that her criticism is based upon love in contrast to the nickles-and-dimes economics of Joe Keller.

We see the implied criticism of the overt idealism most trenchantly through the characterization of Chris Keller, the mouthpiece for the official view. Chris more than any other character in the play talks principles, and it is he who finally drives his father to see that all the fighting men were actually his sons. In pressing Miller's conscious argument to its dramatic crisis, Chris is the voice of the intended theme. "You can be better!" he cries to his parents. "Once and for all you can know there's a universe of people outside and you're responsible to it, and unless you know that you threw away your son because that's why he died." Yet we come to know Chris best not by his overt dramatic role but by his characterization. He is revealed as having all along suspected his father's guilt but as lacking the moral stamina to force the issue. "It's true. I'm yellow. I was made yellow in this house because I suspected my father and I did nothing about it." He has pocketed the profits of the family business along with Joe but held himself morally superior to him. Sue Bayliss acidly remarks that Chris ought to take off his broadcloth if he wants others to don the hair shirt. For the ideals espoused by Chris harass her husband, whom she forced to abandon them. Such revelations seriously compromise the position of the leading character who speaks for the supremacy of the abstract loyalty. If we contrast Chris's damaged position with that of his mother, even though he lectures her, we see that here Miller has made a strong stand for the private in loyalty. The tragedy ends on mother Keller's affirmation as she cries to Chris "Live." Recent history has seemed to endorse Kate's skepticism of slogans. Joe Keller was in error by too closely identifying his clan loyalty with the forty-foot front a business society had drilled into his awareness; Kate Keller's tree is a more compelling symbol.

The final evidence in *All My Sons* for a theme that subverts the obvious intention is the motive for Joe's suicide, the dramatic denouement. Does he really slay himself because he had not until then guessed what Chris so remorsely drives home—that they were all his sons? As he anxiously scans Larry's letter, Joe comments grimly, "Sure, he was my son. But I think to him they were all my sons. And I guess they were, I guess they were." This is surely the key thematic statement of *All My Sons* if the drama is accepted as an expression of the then popular view, that national and even international ideals were superior to family values and that one who failed to see this was indeed a traitor to the democratic one-world just over the shining horizon.

But there is an intimation in this play that the reverse is true—that Joe is a tragic victim because he is betrayed by his sons—by Larry when he abandoned the forty-foot front and by Chris for professing a largely unmerited moral superiority while lining his pockets with the proceeds from a father's life of labor. Joe's aspiration was limited yet sincerely held, one that had been inculcated in him as a supreme virtue by an aggressive society.

How was he to know that in time of war a fluid social pattern could accommodate switches gracefully? Joe's rigidity had been a merit earlier. Is a man wholly to blame for demonstrating the ultimate in selfishness when such a principle has been the ruling passion of those who most command his respect? Is *All My Sons* unequivocal in its final judgment? Is Chris Keller right—Joe betrayed the greater good in serving the smaller? Or is Joe a tragic figure betrayed for clinging to a code that is betrayed by his world? The dialogue indicates quite clearly that the overt message gets home and precipitates Joe's suicide with his admission that all the allied fighting men were his sons. Yet we may legitimately question this seeming clarity.

*All My Sons* may not finally resolve the conflict of antithetical values in time of stress; it is hard to see an easy solution in our contemporary society. What may help obscure the resolution of Miller's play is his own conflict. His unconscious motivation may have got in the way of the more conscious and dramatized message. *All My Sons* concludes upon an ambiguous note but one that is genuinely struck. The play is a success and not a failure. Dramatic success does not wholly hinge upon how clearly the writer saw his problem and how completely he resolved it. A dramatization of our own conflicts seems to me a valid esthetic problem and one that by its very nature may remain less than wholly realized in terms of solution while adequately realized in terms of the dramatic conflict. We ask that the struggle be real and not that technique be supreme.

It is quite possible that when he wrote his play, Arthur Miller felt that local and personal loyalties should justifiably be sacrificed to larger and more nearly universal concepts and ideals. This was the time when an era of good feeling still motivated the former allies in the common front against the fascist repression. Many liberals and some reluctant conservatives were bemused by the intellectual appeal of the popular front through its facile use of slogans. Intellectually Miller may have then gone along for the ride, for it is during this period that the questionable writers' conferences took place; yet the eloquence of Joe and Kate Keller, their dignity and authenticity contrasted with Chris's rather hollow position argue that even then Miller had strong emotional reservations.

One sees the drama then as a realized internal conflict within the artist. This conflict relates to the immemorial strife between clans and their accretions, national states; between the solitary human being and the crystallization and concretion of his dreams. The intellectual Miller spoke through Chris Keller and for the one-world drive; the emotional Miller clung to Kate and Joe Keller. And of course this emotional identification, rather than any strong sympathy for Communist aims, accounts for the playwright's recent refusal to identify certain individuals for the committee investigating alleged subversive activities of some years ago. The dramatist's final and most firm belief is that private loyalties are supreme, despite the siren calls of abstract claims. This is true even in this rather obviously didactic play. *All My Sons* is indeed the symbol for the conscious purpose of the author. But Arthur Miller would affirm the supreme dignity of the private individual and his most immediate loyalties not only against universal slogans and abstractions but as well against his nation's inquisitorial minds and, it goes almost without saying, those of the other ideological camp. He might even violate his own conscious thesis in a play. Only the bigoted or uninformed could hold otherwise. There is ample evidence that in the past decade Arthur Miller has come to hold ever more tenaciously his final commitment, but even so early a play as *All My Sons* carried the seeds of a revolt from its slogans.

# The Living and the Dead in *All My Sons*

*Arvin R. Wells*

Looked at superficially, Arthur Miller's *All My Sons* may appear to be simply a social thesis play. Such classification—a valid one if severely qualified—is suggested both by the timeliness of the story and by the presence of considerable overt social criticism. The story itself is obviously calculated to engage the so-called social conscience. Stated in the simplest terms, the play dramatizes the process by which Joe Keller, a small manufacturer, is forced to accept individual social responsibility and, consequently, to accept his personal guilt for having sold, on one occasion during World War II, fatally defective airplane parts to the government.

However, while this bare-bone synopsis is essentially accurate, it does, in fact, do violence to the actual complexity of the play. In his well-known essay "Tragedy and the Common Man," Miller comments,

> Our lack of tragedy may be partially accounted for by the turn which modern literature has taken toward the purely psychiatric, or purely sociological. . . . From neither of these views can tragedy derive, simply because neither represents a balanced concept of life.

What is reflected here is Miller's own careful avoidance of the "purely" this or that. And it might similarly be said that no satisfactory understanding of Miller's *All My Sons* may be derived from a criticism which commits itself to a "purely" or even predominantly sociological or psychiatric view.

From *Modern Drama* 7, no. 1 (May 1964). © 1964 by the University of Toronto, Graduate Centre for the Study of Drama.

The sociological view is particularly limiting in that it carries with it the temptation to approach the dramatic action from the level of broad socio-cultural generalizations and, consequently, to oversimplify character and action and, stumbling among subtleties of characterization, to accuse the playwright of a confusion of values which belongs appropriately to the characters in their situations.

Actually, like most of Miller's plays, *All My Sons* demands of the reader an awareness of the deviousness of human motivation, an under-standing of the way in which a man's best qualities may be involved in his worst actions and cheapest ideas, and, in general, a peculiarly fine perception of cause and effect. Nowhere is it suggested that the social realities and attitudes that are brought within the critical focus of the play can be honestly considered outside of some such context of human aspirations and weak-nesses as is provided by the play; and nowhere is it suggested that the characters are or can be judged strictly on the basis of some simple social ethic or ideal that might be deduced from the action. The characters do not simply reflect the values and attitudes of a particular society; they use those values and attitudes in their attempt to realize themselves. And it is these characteristics that give *All My Sons,* and other Miller plays, a density of texture so much greater than that of the typical social thesis play, which seeks not only to direct but to facilitate ethical judgments upon matters of topical importance.

For most of us there is no difficulty in assenting to the abstract prop-osition which Chris puts to his mother at the end of the play:

> You can be better! Once and for all you can know now that the
> whole earth comes through those fences; there's a universe out-
> side and you're responsible to it.

And there is no problem either in giving general intellectual assent to the morality of brotherhood for which Chris speaks. There is, however, con-siderable difficulty in assenting to the actual situation at the end of the play, in accepting it as a simple triumph of right over wrong. For the play in its entirety makes clear that Joe Keller has committed his crimes not out of cowardice, callousness, or pure self-interest, but out of a too-exclusive regard for real though limited values, and that Chris, the idealist, is far from acting disinterestedly as he harrows his father to repentance.

Joe Keller is a successful small manufacturer, but he is also "a man whose judgments must be dredged out of experience and a peasant-like common sense." Like many uneducated, self-made men, he has no capacity for abstract considerations; whatever is not personal or at least immediate has no reality for him. He has the peasant's insular loyalty to family which excludes more generalized responsibility to society at large or to mankind in general. At the moment of decision, when his business seemed threatened, the question for him was not basically one of profit and loss; what concerned him was a conflict of responsibilities—his responsibility to his family, particularly his sons to whom the business was to be a legacy of security and joy, versus his responsibility to the unknown men, engaged in the social action of war, who might as a remote consequence suffer for his dishonesty. For such a man as Joe Keller such a conflict could scarcely exist and, given its existence, could have only one probable resolution.

When the worst imaginable consequence follows—twenty-two pilots killed in Australia—Keller is nonetheless able to presume upon his innocence as established before the law. For in his ethical insularity—an insularity stressed in the play by the hedged-in backyard setting—he is safe from any serious assault of conscience so long as he can believe that the family is the most important thing and that what is done in the name of the family has its own justification. Yet, he is not perfectly secure within his sanctuary. His apparently thick skin has its sensitive spots: in his unwillingness to oppose his wife's unhealthy refusal to accept her son Larry's death, in his protest against Ann Deever's rejection of her father, in his insistence that he does not believe in "crucifying a man," and in his insistence that Chris should use what he, the father, has earned, "with joy . . . without shame . . . with joy," he betrays a deep-seated fear. His appeal on behalf of Herb Deever (act 1) is in fact, partly a covert appeal on his own behalf, an appeal for merciful understanding called forth by the shocked realization that some considerations may override and even destroy the ties of family upon which his own security rests.

It is Chris Keller who, in reaching out for love and a life of his own, first undermines and then destroys this security altogether. Chris has brought out of the war an idealistic morality of brotherhood based on what he has seen of mutual self-sacrifice among the men whom he commanded. But he has not survived the war unwounded; he bears a still festering psychological wound, a sense of inadequacy and guilt. He has survived to enjoy the fruits of a wartime economy, and he fears that in enjoying them he becomes unworthy, condemned by his own idealism. Even his love for Ann Deever, the sweetheart of his dead brother, has seemed to him a guilty desire to take advantage of the dead to whom he somehow owes his life.

As the play opens, however, he has decided to assert himself to claim the things in life and the position in life which he feels should rightfully be his, and as the initial step he has invited Ann to his family home. His decision brings him into immediate conflict with his mother, Kate Keller, who looks upon the possible marriage between Chris and Ann as a public confirmation of Larry's death. At first Joe Keller seems only peripherally involved in this conflict; his attempt to evade Chris's demand that Kate be forced to accept Larry's death carries only ambiguous suggestions of insecurity. However, at the end of act 2, Kate, emotionally exhausted by the fruitless effort to use George Deever's accusations as a means of driving out Ann, and opposed for the first time by the declared disbelief of both husband and son, breaks down and reveals the actual basis of her refusal: if Chris lets Larry go, then he must let his father go as well. What is revealed here is that Kate is fundamentally like her husband; only what is personal or immediate is real for her. If Larry is alive, then, in a sense, the war has no reality, and Joe's crimes do not mean anything; their consequences are merely distant echoes in an unreal world. But if Larry is dead, then the war is real, and Joe is guilty of murder, even, by an act of association, guilty of murdering his own son. Her own desperate need to reject Larry's death against all odds and upon whatever flimsy scrap of hope has been the reflex of her need to defend her relation to her husband against whatever in herself might be outraged by the truth about him. Actually, however, Kate has "an overwhelming capacity for love" and an ultimate commitment to the living which makes it possible for her to "let Larry go" and rise again to the defense of her husband at the end. It is Larry living not Larry dead that she clings to, and she does this because to admit his death would make both life and love more difficult. Moreover, as is generally true of Miller's important women, Kate's final loyalty is to her husband; to him as a living, substantial being, she, like Linda in *Death of a Salesman,* has made an irrevocable commitment in love and sympathy which no knowledge *about* him can destroy.

Chris, on the other hand, is incapable of any such surrender of the letter of morality in the name of love or mercy; he cannot, as his father would have him, "see it human." At the rise of the curtain in act 2, Chris is seen dragging away the remains of Larry's memorial tree. The action is clearly symbolic; Chris, because of his own needs, has determined to free the family of the shadow of self-deception and guilt cast over it by the memory of Larry, to let in the light of truth. Yet, when the light comes, he is less able to bear it than the others. Ann, in the hope of love and marriage, rejects the seeds of hatred and remorse which her brother, George, offers her, and Kate sacrifices the dead son to the living father. But Chris has too much at stake; his life must vindicate the deaths of those who died in the war, which means that he must maintain an ideal image of himself or else be overwhelmed by his own sense of guilt. Because he is closely identified with his father, his necessary sense of personal dignity and worthiness depends upon his belief in the ideal image of his father; consequently, he can only accept the father's exposure as a personal defeat.

It becomes clear in the exchange between Chris and George Deever (act 2) that Chris has suspected his father but has suppressed his suspicions because he could not face the consequences—the condemnation of the father, whom he loves, and the condemnation of himself as polluted by sharing in the illicit spoils of war. Yet, this is precisely what the exposure of Joe Keller forces upon him, and Joe's arguments in self-defense—that he had expected the defective parts to be rejected, that what he did was done for the family, that business is business and none of it is "clean"—all shatter upon the hard shell of Chris's idealism not simply because they are, in fact, evasions and irrelevant half-truths, but because they cannot satisfy Chris's conscience. Consequently, even after Larry's suicide letter has finally brought to Joe a realization of his personal responsibility, Chris must go on to insist upon a public act of penance. The father becomes, indeed, a kind of scapegoat for the son; that is, if Joe expiates his crimes through the acceptance of a just punishment, then Chris will be relieved of his own burden of paralyzing guilt. His love of his father and his complicity with his father will then no longer imply his own unworthiness. In insisting that Joe must go to prison, Chris is, in effect, asking Joe to give him back his self-respect, so that he may be free to marry Ann and assume the life which is rightfully his. But Chris's inability to accept his father "as a man" leads Joe to believe that not only have his defenses crumbled but that the whole basis of his life is gone, and he kills himself.

Because it forces upon the reader an awareness of the intricacies of human motivation and of human relationships, *All My Sons* leaves a dual impression: the action affirms the theme of the individual's responsibility to humanity, but, at the same time, it suggests that the standpoint of even so fine an ideal is not an altogether adequate one from which to evaluate human beings, and that a rigid idealism operating in the actual world of men entails suffering and waste, especially when the idealist is hagridden by his own ideals. There is no simple opposition here between those "who know" and those who "must learn," between those who possess the truth and those who have failed to grasp it, between the spiritually well and the spiritually sick. Moreover, the corruption and destruction of a man like Joe Keller, who is struggling to preserve what he conceives to be a just evaluation of himself in the eyes of his son, implies, in the context of the play, a deficiency not only in Keller's character but in the social environment in which he exists. Keller's appeal to the general ethics of the business community—

> If my money's dirty there ain't a clean nickel in the United States. Who worked for nothin' in that war? . . . Did they ship a gun or a truck outa Detroit before they got their price? . . . It's dollars and cents, nickels and dimes; war and peace, it's nickels and dimes, what's clean?

—is irrelevant to his personal defense; yet, it is an indictment of that community nonetheless. For it indicates that the business community failed to provide any substantial values which might have supplemented and counterbalanced Keller's own limited, family-based ethics. From the business community came only the impulse to which Chris also responds when he feels prompted to express his love for Ann by saying, "I'm going to make a fortune for you!"

Furthermore, there is a sense in which Kate's words, "We were all struck by the same lightning," are true; the lightning was the experience of the Second World War—a massive social action in which they were all, willy-nilly, involved. It was the war that made it possible for some to profit by the suffering and death of others and that created the special occasion of Joe Keller's temptation, which led in turn to his son Larry's suicide and his wife's morbid obsession. Chris Keller and George Deever brought something positive out of the war—an ideal of brotherhood and a firmer, more broadly based ethic—but George, as he appears in the play, is paying in remorse for the principles that led him to reject his father, and Chris's idealism is poisoned at the source by shame and guilt, which are also products of his war experience and which make it impossible for him to temper justice with mercy either for himself or anyone else.

# Miller, Ibsen, and Organic Drama

*Sheila Huftel*

"You have such a talent for ignoring things." This exasperated accusation is made by Chris in *All My Sons,* which, like Miller's adaptation of *An Enemy of the People,* deals with the clash between people who can and people who cannot walk away from things. Both plays are about evasion and commitment, a wilful blindness and a need to see. Joe Keller and Peter Stockmann can settle for an unprincipled practicality; Chris and Dr. Stockmann cannot.

Keller protests, in excuse, "Chris, a man can't be a Jesus in this world!" It is meaningless to Chris: without his commitment there would be no person left. Through Jim Bayliss, Miller shows what would have become of Chris had he followed the "practicality" urged on him. Jim was a doctor committed to research who imagined that he could give it up, accept a small-town practice, and not be lost. He is, in fact, destroyed far more deeply than Keller. "These private little revolutions always die. The compromise is always made . . . and now I live in the usual darkness; I can't find myself; and it is even hard sometimes to remember the kind of man I wanted to be." But for Miller compromise is not obligatory, and in these plays it is rarely made. Chris, Willy Loman, John Proctor, the helplessly driven Eddie Carbone, all preserve their selfhood by standing out against Jim's assumption; it is the compromises made in *After the Fall* that cripple Quentin.

From *Arthur Miller: The Burning Glass.* © 1965 by Sheila Huftel. Citadel Press, 1965. Published by arrangement with Lyle Stuart.

The time of the play is just after the war and Chris embodies Miller's argument:

> Everything was being destroyed, see, but it seemed to me that one new thing was being made. A kind of responsibility. Man for man. You understand me? To show that, to bring that onto the earth again like some kind of monument and everyone would feel it standing there, behind him, and it would make a difference to him. And then I came home and it was incredible. I—there was no meaning in it here; the whole thing to them was some kind of bus accident. I went to work for Dad and that rat-race again. I felt—what you said—ashamed somehow. Because nobody was changed at all. It seemed to make suckers out of a lot of guys. I felt all wrong to be alive, to open a bank-book, to drive the new car, to see the new refrigerator. I mean you can take those things out of a war, but when you drive that car you've got to know that it came out of the love a man can have for a man. You've got to be a little better because of that. Otherwise what you have is really loot, and there's blood on it.

Chris's belief seems to have grown out of a long line of experience. During the war Miller was asked to go round the camps and training centers of America to find the material for a true war film—only the facts, shorn of all fiction. Miller did not complete the script for *The Story of G.I. Joe,* but published what he had found in *Situation Normal.* . . . It is a sensitive book and through it Miller is driven by the need to define a belief that will make sense of the war. "Something besides horror must be proved, or only horror will remain." He was concerned with the individual behind the uniform, with the kind of world the soldier would be coming back to and what would happen if he was disappointed.

Some aspects of the book seem to influence *All My Sons* and especially the full drawing of Watson. Through his heroism in the Pacific, Watson had been chosen for officers' training and sent home. He had found it hard to leave the island because he knew that "everybody had a right to go and wanted to."

His home town gave him a big demonstration and made him a hero. He talked with Miller mainly to ensure that there would be no mistakes in the film. "I liked it at the beginning," he told him, "but Jesus Christ, the real heroes never come back. They're the real ones. They're the only ones. Nobody's a hero if he can still breathe. . . . I mean I don't want to cheat so many dead men."

Watson spoke of the friendship out there, and his loyalty is reflected in Chris. When he tells Ann about the company he lost, he says in effect: "Friendship is the greatest thing out there. I mean real friendship, not because a guy can give you what you want. I tell you the truth: I would die for any one of the thirty or forty men out there just as easy as I'd flick out this match. I swear this is the truth. I don't expect you to believe it, but I swear it."

By contrast, Watson was alone in America. He was not doing well at the training camp and seemed not to have the intellectual ability for the courses. His dread was that if he failed he could not go home or back to the front. He did not know what he was going to do.

Miller understood the debt Watson felt, and in explaining him wondered what would become of the countless Watsons coming home to an America not conscious of nor fighting for its belief. "Half of him, in a sense, must die." He would have had a place in the struggle for a belief. "It would demand that part of his character which requires sharing. As it is, the company is gone and all that the company meant. He must wall himself from his fellow man, he must live only his own little life and do his own unimportant, unsatisfying job when he gets out of the Army. He must begin again the stale and deadly competition with his fellow men for rewards which now seem colorless, even if necessary for his survival. He is alone. Cut off from mankind and the great movement of mankind he was once part of. And the world is alien." Miller predicted that Watson "will be wondering why he went and why he is alive for the rest of his days." And this is the position Chris holds in the play. The difference is that through Chris, Miller defines the "idea" growing among the soldiers.

Miller wrote *Situation Normal . . .* when he was twenty-seven, and the book is rather like a young photograph. He remains concerned with how the world can be made less alien; we will meet this concern again over Willy Loman. In *After the Fall* Quentin, outside the concentration camp, nails the idea behind *Situation Normal . . .* to one line: "And I without belief stand here disarmed."

The idea of *All My Sons* was in the air—almost, it must have seemed, tangible. The details of the plot were fact. Miller was told of a family in which the daughter discovered that her father had sold defective machinery to the army, and she handed him over to the authorities. All Miller's plays are rooted in reality. It is part of his ambition to write plays for common-sense people, and ensures that his ideas will not float about like ghosts who have permanently lost their haunting-ground. His plays are built as though he were constructing skyscrapers, not scenes. He says in his preface [to the

*Collected Plays*] that he desired above all to write rationally, and adds: "I have always been in love with wonder, the wonder of how people got to be the way they are." Wonder, for Miller, is something essentially explicable, a logic of people and events caused by "the gradual and remorseless crush of factual and psychological conflict."

This is the basis of *All My Sons* and of all Miller's flesh-and-blood social drama. Keller killed twenty-one pilots during the war by shipping defective airplane parts, for which his partner was jailed. Nothing could be more clear cut; so far it is cardboard drama. But these people are involved in a forest of mutual and parallel relationships, and the play is so balanced that if Chris's relationship with his father is not fully established, half the play is lost. The relationships in *All My Sons* make it the dramatic equivalent of the plot of *Bleak House*. Chris loves his parents and, although haunted by his brother's death, plans to marry Larry's fiancée, who is also the daughter of the jailed partner. The marriage is guaranteed to upset his mother because it confirms her son's death, something she cannot accept, sensing that if Larry is dead Keller is responsible. Chris is parallel to Frank, a practical opportunist, to George, the jailed man's son, and to Jim. He relates to every character in the play.

Miller carries this relatedness through from people to events; it is the foundation on which *All My Sons* is built. "Joe Keller's trouble . . . is not that he cannot tell right from wrong but that his cast of mind cannot admit that he, personally, has any viable connection with his world, his universe, or his society" (preface, *Collected Plays*). Miller shies away from the obvious "crime" element in the play, the selling of defective airplane parts. That is too simple. It does not say enough. To Miller that would be the plot of a thriller, a meaningless kill-time. Having generously bequeathed the plot to the American counterpart of Agatha Christie, in his preface he defines what his play is about: "The fortress which *All My Sons* lays siege to is the fortress of unrelatedness. It is an assertion not so much of a morality in terms of right and wrong, but of the moral world's being such because men cannot walk away from certain of their deeds." Relatedness and responsibility. The central problem of the play is to bring the fact home to Joe Keller, to batter down the opaque glass walls of his isolation. Miller is concerned with consciousness, not crime, and with bringing a man face to face with the consequences he has caused, forcing him to share in the results of his creation.

He is not a chess-playing dramatist, a manipulator of black and white pieces of wood hierarchically designed. Keller literally stands for the world that Chris has come back to, self-centered and unseeing. But Miller cares too much for his people to reduce them to ciphers; with Keller he wins his argument, but without crucifying the man. Keller is committed only to his family, and can see no further—nothing beyond that. Miller's drawing is always compassionate, and the man is so drawn that the general concepts of his son are outside the range of his understanding. His limitation is explained: "A heavy man of stolid mind and build . . . but the imprint of the machine-shop worker and boss still upon him. When he reads, when he speaks, when he listens, it is with the terrible concentration of the uneducated man for whom there is still wonder in many commonly known things, a man whose judgments must be dredged out of experience and a peasantlike common sense."

Keller illustrates Miller's belief that an idea is no guide to the man holding it until you know why he believes as he does. Keller's vulnerable position makes him appear more liberal than Ann when he, naturally, protests against her attack on her father: "I never believed in crucifying people." It is himself he is defending. Chris sees the facts; the man killed twenty-one pilots. There is nothing to add, and he drives Keller to his only defense: "A father is a father!" Miller adds a stage direction to deepen understanding of Keller; he has been particularly careful over him: "As though the outburst revealed him, he looks about, wanting to retract it."

The insights Keller does have are nervelessly bludgeoning and accurate. His partner was "a little man . . . always scared of loud voices." Finally, this rock-solid egocentric is desperate and alone, alone in his version of what he has done. Baffled in the extreme, he still tries to blink facts by reaching for his family. His plea is a general one: "Then what do I do? Tell me, talk to me, what do I do?" Kate cannot help him, except to warn: "You want to live? You better figure out your life." Unrepentant, he argues that nothing is bigger than the family: "There's nothing he could do that I wouldn't forgive. Because he's my son. Because I'm his father and he's my son . . . and if there's something bigger than that I'll put a bullet in my head." In spite of the family, in spite of the generally accepted code of practicality—"Who worked for nothin' in that war?"—his self-justification breaks. It breaks on the realization that Larry deliberately crashed his plane, so making his father directly responsible for his death. And with final realization, Keller kills himself.

Miller draws his minor characters with a precision that tells you only what you need to know. This can make them appear underdrawn until you notice how meticulously they reveal themselves. Frank, who believes in fortune-telling by the stars, accuses Jim: "The trouble with you is, you don't *believe* in anything." Sue resents "living next door to the Holy Family.

It makes me look like a bum, you understand?" George, Ann's brother, has a deeply felt sense of relationships: "I wanted to go to Dad and tell him you were going to be married. It seemed impossible not to tell him. He loved you so much. . . . Annie, you don't know what was done to that man. You don't know what happened." This passionate concern for the individual is expressed in all Miller's plays.

Miller's realism is the strength of his characters. The Kellers live on and are consoled by the heroism of their dead son, particularly the mother. Miller describes her as "a woman of uncontrolled inspirations and an over-whelming capacity for love." Kate is too sensitive to stare past facts like Keller. She wraps herself in dreams and from this phantom comfort tries to will Larry back to life by faith. Miller explores the reasons for Kate's delusion—her sickness, her being driven to clutch at mysticism and as-trology—and at bottom discovers a genuine faith in a moral order. "Your brother's alive, darling, because if he's dead, your father killed him. Do you understand now? . . . God does not let a son be killed by his father."

Kate has to believe it. But when the dream breaks she protects Keller. Most often there is resilience in Miller's dreamers. The person comes through and they are not allowed to wander far from reality. (Willy Loman's tragedy is that he is overaware of things as they are, and that they contradict his longing.) Look at the ghost-haunted Kellers: "We're like at a railroad station waiting for a train that never comes in." And yet they are not pseudo-Hamlets, nor do they search for their egos in a mental looking glass. Every-day things crowd in upon them and in this welter of triviality there is no time for tragic grief. Day-to-day living never leaves Miller's characters alone. Choosing between Aldous Huxley's "Tragedy and the Whole Truth," he chooses the whole truth. The whole truth admits all the facts and irrelevancies that in life temper situations and characters; tragedy ex-cludes them because they diminish its height and purity. The whole truth forbids Kate to languish in grief. She comes out into daylight and tries to prevent Chris from jailing Keller: "The war is over! Didn't you hear? It's over!" However moving, because coming from her, Chris reminds her that Larry didn't kill himself so that she and Keller could be "sorry."

> KATE: What more can we be?
> CHRIS: You can be better! Once and for all you can know
>     there's a universe of people outside and you're
>     responsible to it, and unless you know that, you threw
>     away your son because that's why he died.

As often happens with Miller's plays, his intention was contradicted by its reception in New York. In the face of Miller's denial the press insisted that the play was theatrical and praised it accordingly (all but Robert Coleman, of the *Daily Mirror,* who lived up to the tough New York critic's reputation by complaining that the play was underwritten and the people placid: I have visions of him living on a steady diet of pale playwrights and drinking molten lead). Miller stressed that the play was intended to be as untheatrical and artless as possible; but his natural talent cheated him. To Miller, it appears, "theatrical" is suspect praise. In his preface he said: "It began to seem to me that what I had written until then, as well as almost all the plays I had ever seen, had been written for a theatrical performance, when they should have been written as a kind of testimony whose relevance far surpassed theatrics."

In writing about Miller, people seem impelled to oversimplify him, arriving at a clear-cut half-man, half-truth. He denies the role thrust upon him of abstract moralist—talkative upon a peak in Darien. "*All My Sons* has often been called a moral play, but the concept of morality is not quite as purely ethical as it has been made to appear, nor is it so in the plays that follow" (preface, *Collected Plays*). Put it this way: Miller is concerned with why people live the way they do; he is a builder with available materials rather than an architect hawking blueprints for an ideal house.

*All My Sons* is fervent early Miller, a step away from *Situation Normal. . . .* The voice is authentic and arresting, the technique still stiff with its newness—for instance in the contrived discovery of the letter—and from time to time the key is too high, like a singer uncertain of pitch. The dialogue is alternately collar-gripping or wryly ironic. A new light was thrown on the ending by a friend who knew nothing of the play, but arrived in time to catch the last few minutes of it on television. A shot is heard from the house, and in the final scene Chris is being comforted by Kate. Without even asking what the play was about, he said: "It looks like something straight out of Dostoevsky." Perhaps he was more right than he knew. Miller was steeped in Dostoevsky at that time.

Miller in *All My Sons* has been carelessly labeled "Ibsenite" and an immutable pattern has been set up. People who use labels are like a man capable of seeing ten miles, swearing that he can see only five because that is as far as he expects to see. Let us ignore "Ibsenite" as a shortcut to defining Miller and concentrate on Ibsen's influence upon him, which is not the same thing. One writer's influence on another does not create a blood-discipleship, and should not, unless the second is to become a carbon copy of the first. The differences between the two writers are too obvious to need retelling, but let us trace their connection.

There is a certain like-mindedness between them. Some lines in Ibsen's letters could well have come from Miller, and I suspect they would find common ground in Ibsen's speech to the Norwegian students on September 10, 1874:

> It was a long time before I realized that to be a poet means essentially to see; but mark well, to see in such a way that whatever is seen is perceived by his audience just as the poet saw it. But only what has been lived through can be seen in that way and accepted in that way. And the secret of modern literature lies precisely in this matter of experiences that have been personally lived through. All that I have written these last ten years I have lived through in spirit. But no poet lives through anything in isolation. What he lives through, all his countrymen live through with him. If that were not so, what would bridge the gap between the creating and the receiving mind?

Miller would probably agree with this definition of insight as the importance of seeing and truth of reporting. His plays reflect his experience, always in relation to his time, and that time to a general truth. The "Now" of the plays is like a stone flung into water that rings around it. Miller's concern is as much with the rings as with the stone; with its effect as well as its impact. His concern is with causes, actions, and the consequences of actions. He sees beyond the present fact which often blinds his audience, with the result that appreciation of his plays grows as time distances them. This happened with *The Crucible* and will happen with *After the Fall*. Then his relationship with his audience proves that he, too, believes that nothing is lived through in isolation.

Miller admits turning to Ibsen with a sense of homecoming. Here was an organic drama of fact, a synthesis of person and action, of fact with feeling, instead of their isolation. Miller had been immersed in drama of feeling at that time and had come to distrust it. It is possible that Ibsen helped make some of his ideas articulate for him. There is, somehow, excitement and elation in the recognition he felt: "I saw . . . his ability to forge a play upon a factual bedrock. A situation in his plays is never stated but revealed in terms of hard actions, irrevocable deeds; and sentiment is never confused with the action it conceals" (preface, *Collected Plays*). Miller holds this same balance in *All My Sons* and through all his plays.

When Arthur Miller adapted *An Enemy of the People* in 1950, he wrote in his introduction: "Ibsen's profound source of strength . . . is his insistence, his utter conviction, that he is going to say what he has to say, and the audience, by God, is going to listen. It is the very same quality that makes a star actor, a great public speaker and a lunatic."

It is certain that Miller found Ibsen's outlook an inspiration. Miller also wrote in his introduction that "Now listen here!" gave him a way out and went on to deplore the state of neon-lit fiction which must have appealed to him like spun sugar to a diabetic. "It has become the fashion for plays to reduce the thickness of life to a fragile facsimile, to avoid portraying the complexities of life, the contradictions of character, the fascinating interplay of cause and effect that have long been part of the novel." His interpretation is wide as the world; and we are in fact planets away from "Now listen here," which usually means that an argument is to be heard, and "thickness" can be fragile to transparency. Again, this is the wholeness in Miller, that wholeness he admired in Ibsen.

Miller took this up again in his preface, and Ibsen's technique seemed specially designed to fit Miller's ambition to bring to the stage the density of the novel. To achieve this a play must accept and reflect change and development; otherwise it suggests that people and situations are static. Then once characters are mutilated to fit the present, the all-important explanation is left unmade. So concerned was Ibsen with documenting and dramatizing the past that it is the past that is alive. In *The Master Builder* Solness is only half burnt out, but in *John Gabriel Borkman* the past takes total possession and the characters really "died" twenty years before. This is Ibsen at his most surrealist—the dead are talking with the dead. "I think too many modern plays assume," said Miller, "that their duty is merely to show the present countenance rather than to account for what happens."

Miller believes that drama can never attain full consciousness until the past can be contrasted with the present and the audience made aware of how the present has become what it is. Simply and directly, *All My Sons* accounts for what happens; but both *Death of a Salesman* and *After the Fall* are built toward full consciousness, with a living contrast between past and present. This grows out of Miller's definition of the value of Ibsen to him: "What is precious in the Ibsen method is its insistence upon valid causation. . . . This is the 'real' in Ibsen's realism for me, for he was . . . as much a mystic as a realist, which is simply to say that while there are mysteries in life which no amount of analyzing will reduce to reason, it is perfectly realistic to admit and even to proclaim that hiatus as a truth. But the problem is not to make complex what is essentially explainable; it is to make understandable what is complex without distorting and oversimplifying what cannot be explained" (preface, *Collected Plays*). On that the balance of Miller's plays rest.

"No, don't walk around it" sets the mood for the adaptation of *An Enemy of the People,* as it did for *All My Sons.* Both plays are essentially about evasion. Miller sums up definitively by adding a line not in the Archer translation. Stockmann's two boys have been sent home from school after one of them was hurt in a fight.

> EJLIF: They started calling you names, so he got sore and
>     began to fight with one kid, and all of a sudden a whole
>     bunch of them—
> MRS. STOCKMANN: Why did you answer?
> MORTEN: They called him a traitor! My father is no traitor!
> EJLIF: *But you didn't have to answer!*
>
>                                                   (my italics)

The whole play turns on the fact that you do have to answer.

"The whole cast of his [Ibsen's] thinking was such that he could not have lived a day under an authoritarian regime of any kind." And neither could Miller. The main conflict of the play is between the individual and authority. "Simply, it is a question of whether the democratic guarantees protecting political minorities ought to be set aside in time of crisis. More personally, it is a question of whether one's vision of the truth ought to be a source of guilt at a time when the mass of men condemn it as a dangerous and devilish lie . . . because there never was, nor will there ever be, an organized society able to countenance calmly the individual who insists that he is right while the vast majority is absolutely wrong" (introduction, *An Enemy of the People*).

Stockmann is just such an individual. He insists that the water at the newly built health springs is poisoned; this has been scientifically proved. It is the truth. All at once he is made the figurehead of a progressive revolution, with the backing of the liberal majority—until his discovery affects the town's pocket. The Mayor, his brother, threatens a new tax to pay for the rebuilding, which will take two years. In the face of the new tax and lean years, it is convenient to believe Peter that Stockmann's report "is based on vindictiveness, on his hatred of authority and nothing else. This is the mad dream of a man who is trying to blow up your way of life! It has nothing to do with reform or science or anything else, but pure and simple destruction." In mob vs. man Stockmann is branded a traitor. Truth is made irrelevant and shied away from as if it were a disease.

The play reflects Ibsen's anger over the Norwegian reaction to *Ghosts*. He wrote to Georg Brandes, January 3, 1882: "And what can be said of the attitude assumed by the so-called liberal press—of those leaders of the people who speak and write of freedom of action and thought but at the same time make themselves slaves to the supposed opinions of their subscribers?"

It must have seemed to Ibsen that there was always a stupid, savage crowd somewhere, ready to tear a man apart, and Stockmann stands out against that crowd in the most resounding defense of individualism in all drama. His meeting has been taken away from him, but at least he is given permission to speak, provided he does not mention the poisoned springs. But by now he has found a new truth: "Don't think you can fog up my brain with that magic word—the People! Not any more! Just because there is a mass of organisms with the human shape, they do not automatically become a people. That honor has to be earned! Nor does one automatically become a Man by having human shape, and living in a house, and feeding one's face—and agreeing with one's neighbors. That name *also* has to be earned. . . . Before many can know something, *one* must know it! It's always the same. Rights are sacred until it hurts for somebody to use them." F. L. Lucas, in his book *Ibsen and Strindberg,* suggested that a national theatre could best educate its public by performing *An Enemy of the People* every year.

Ibsen's anger carried his Stockmann toward fascism: and here, Miller thought, had come the time to cut. The play lies somewhere between the ring and the circus. Anger inspires it and the dialogue is flung down like a challenge—"What am I not going to do?" It is the dramatist's equivalent of the circus high wire; a man is about to get his life broken. The words presage personal disasters; a variation of them led to the blinding of Oedipus and the stoning of Brand.

Basically, Stockmann is Miller's committed man, who cannot compromise. He is told that he could have everything—except the truth. That "everything" he sees as nothing, and he confirms his isolation and suffers the social and economic consequences for himself and his family. Not all Ibsen's fighters are seen from this angle and found right. *The Wild Duck* was written as a warning against absolute truth when the price is inflated. Gregers Werle's progress is reflected in lives breaking like egg shells around him, and Brand remains a warning against total commitment to an abstract ideal, however high.

Stockmann has been carefully drawn to avoid a voice-through-a-megaphone reformer. There is an uncertainty about him, his manner is confused, and even, on occasion, lost. He has doubts, enthusiasms, and nerves. He is impractical to the verge of innocence. Chaplinesque is the situation as he visits the editor who is about to print his report on the Springs. Hotfoot with excitement, he has come to see the proofs, and—

> STOCKMANN: Just walking down the street now, I looked at
> the people, in the stores, driving the wagons, and
> suddenly I was—well, touched, you know? By their
> innocence, I mean. What I'm driving at is, when this
> exposé breaks, they're liable to start making a saint out of
> me or something, and I—Aslaksen, I want you to
> promise me that you're not going to try to get up any
> dinner for me or—
> ASLAKSEN: Doctor, there's no use concealing—
> STOCKMANN: I knew it. Now look, I will simply not attend a
> dinner in my honor.

What there was no use concealing was that Peter had talked them out of printing the report, and that Stockmann was to be broken by his former friends.

In an interesting production of the play at Lincoln by John Hale, George Coulouris played Stockmann as bovine and avuncular. He was a man capable of being converted to any cause, a sleep-writing pamphleteer. Certainly this is a possible interpretation that underlines the fact that Stockmann is not necessarily always right. There is an element of "good fellow" in Stockmann that Miller has preserved and even accentuated, and it is this that Mr. Coulouris stressed. He was a bewildered man who obstinately knew he was right, and was holding firmly to that knowledge. His interpretation gave Peter grounds for impatience. But, for me, he was the wrong kind of man with the wrong kind of enthusiasm.

The fact of the matter is, regardless of how intelligent Miller makes Stockmann and of any personal preference, George Coulouris did play the Stockmann Ibsen intended. In the preface to the Archer edition (1907), you will find this extract from Ibsen's letter to Hegel: "But the Doctor is a more muddleheaded person than I am, and he has, moreover, several other characteristics because of which people will stand hearing a good many things from him which they might perhaps not have taken in such very good part had they been said by me." Ibsen, of all people, choosing the screen of stupidity! Mr. Coulouris is content with Ibsen's Stockmann; Machiavelli aside, I prefer Miller's. He is a man of greater mind, of more dynamic intelligence, who has ideas going off in his head like firecrackers. He is altogether less fussy and more colorfully self-dramatizing. With him the play has more edge, greater drive, and sharper impact.

I doubt if Miller could have drawn Stockmann any other way, partly, perhaps, because he has more sympathy with commitment than Ibsen. This

Stockmann is naturally Miller's hero, by temperament and intellect. Then the time at which he was writing probably influenced him at least as much as the reception of *Ghosts* influenced Ibsen. It is possible that during McCarthyism Miller had no wish to disguise his Stockmann.

Stockmann believed: "On the wreckage of all the civilizations in the world there ought to be a big sign, 'They didn't dare!' " Ibsen's clash between the Individual and Authority was as pertinent when Miller adapted it as when it was written. Even in minor aspects it was alive. Miller's Stockmann, after being declared "an enemy of the people," says: "I bet if I walked down the street now not one of them would admit he ever met me!" That was real enough; seven years later, Miller wrote in his preface to the *Collected Plays:* "Astounded, I watched men pass me by without a nod whom I had known rather well for years."

# The Failure of Social Vision

*Edward Murray*

*All My Sons* (1947), which earned Miller the [New York] Drama Critics' Circle Award for the season, is a tightly constructed three-act play. In his introduction to the *Collected Plays,* Miller has explained his purposes in the following manner:

> The form of *All My Sons* is a reflection and expression of several forces. . . . I desired above all to write rationally. . . . If there is one word to name the mood I felt it was *Forego.* Let nothing interfere with the shape, the direction, the intention. . . . My intention . . . was to be as untheatrical as possible. To that end any metaphor, any image, any figure of speech, however creditable to me, was removed if it even slightly brought to consciousness the hand of a writer. So far as was possible nothing was to be permitted to interfere with its artlessness. . . . I wanted then to write so that people of common sense would mistake my play for life itself and not be required to lend it some poetic license before it could be believed. I wanted to make the moral world as real and evident as the immoral one so splendidly is.

The time-sequence in *All My Sons* covers less than twenty-four hours: act 1 opens "early Sunday morning"; act 2 begins "that evening"; and act 3 commences at "Two o'clock the following morning." There is a single setting: the backyard of the Keller family "in the outskirts of an American

From *Arthur Miller, Dramatist.* © 1967 by Frederick Ungar Publishing Co., Inc.

town." Action proceeds along a single line, culminating in a climactic explosion.

In act 1, Miller is at pains to set the stage carefully for the action which follows. Thus, about the first half of the opening act is merely introductory in nature. Miller's strategy here is to focus steadily on Joe Keller as a prosperous businessman, devoted husband and father, and friendly neighbor. As Joe reclines in his yard, scanning the Sunday papers and talking to his neighbors, he emerges as a simple but shrewd man of middle age, whose eldest son, Larry, was reported missing during the Second World War, and whose wife, Kate, influenced by a neighbor's horoscope, refuses to believe that Larry is dead. The younger son, Chris, who returned safely from the war has invited Ann, Larry's old girlfriend, to visit the Kellers. When Chris informs Joe that he plans to marry Ann, Joe warns his son that if he does so it will destroy Kate's dream that Larry will one day return. Conflict is focused sharply when Chris threatens to take Ann to New York. This upsets Joe because the move will be a rejection of the Keller business, and the business means everything to Joe. Each of the three chief characters, then—Joe, Kate, and Chris—is seen to have something vital at stake. In the introduction various suggestions are made about a guilty secret in Joe's past, but the problem becomes more than a vague hint when Kate objects to a game that Joe is playing with a neighbor's boy, a game that Kate calls a "jail business" one, and Joe, "alarmed" and "angered," asks: "What have I got to hide?" To this Kate replies: "I didn't say you had anything to hide." This is the point of attack, which occurs slightly past the middle of act 1, for, although conflict is foreshadowed earlier, the major dramatic question—Joe's probable guilt—is unmistakably pointed to here for the first time. Miller has said:

> Its first act was later called slow, but it was designed to be slow.
> It was made so that even boredom might threaten, so that when
> the first intimation of the crime is dropped a genuine horror
> might begin to move into the heart of the audience . . . born of
> the contrast between the placidity of the civilization on view and
> the threat to it that a rage of conscience could create.
>
> (introduction to the *Collected Plays*)

This problem will be discussed below in my criticism of the structure.

In the last half of act 1, Ann appears and informs Kate that she has stopped waiting for Larry to return. Kate, however, remains inflexible in her belief. Exposition reveals that Joe and Ann's father had both been in jail for shipping defective airplane parts during the war, an action which resulted in the deaths of twenty-one American pilots, but that Joe had managed to get exonerated by claiming to be ill at home the day that the parts were shipped. Ann's father, however, remained in prison. Chris and Ann, who consider Ann's father a murderer, cannot understand Joe's tolerant attitude toward his former partner. Chris is especially critical on the subject because his conscience troubles him about his returning alive from the war when so many of his company died in combat. Ann assures Chris, however, that he has a right to happiness. The curtain descends on an ominous note with the report that George, Ann's brother, after visiting his father in jail, is coming to visit the Kellers.

Conflict rises in act 2 when George accuses Joe of being guilty of the crime which has ruined George's family. The Kellers manage to placate George, and for a little while the situation seems more promising for the Kellers. It is Kate, finally, who destroys the pretense of Joe's innocence when she blunders and says: "[Joe] hasn't been laid up in fifteen years." This "slip of the tongue" reveals the deception that Joe has perpetrated, and from this revelation—which is the turning point of the play—various effects swiftly result. George demands that Ann leave the house with him, and Kate, for her own reasons, agrees with George. When Chris refuses to part from Ann, Kate says:

> Your brother's alive, darling, because if he's dead, your father
> killed him. . . . God does not let a son be killed by his father.
> Now you see, don't you?

Chris then confronts Joe with the dramatic question suggested in act 1 at the point of attack: "Then . . . you did it?" Presently Joe confesses, and the curtain falls on a confused Chris: "What must I do . . . what must I do?"

In act 3, Joe tells Kate: "If there's something bigger than [the family] I'll put a bullet in my head!" This line is preparation for Joe's suicide six and a half pages later. According to Joe, Larry was not like Chris; Larry was "practical": "To him the world had a forty-foot front, it ended at the building line." Ann enters, announces that she will not expose Joe, but insists that Kate release Chris from feeling "guilty with me." When Kate refuses, Ann declares that Larry is dead. After sending Joe into the house, Ann produces a letter which was written by Larry on the day that he died. Chris enters with Joe and it is related that Chris hesitates to deliver Joe to justice because the business world shares the guilt with Joe. After reading

Larry's letter, however, Chris changes his mind, for the letter reveals that Larry was not so "practical" as Joe had supposed. This is the crisis of the play. In the letter, Larry says:

> They flew in a load of papers from the States and I read about Dad and your father being convicted. . . . I can't bear to live any more. . . . How could he have done that? Every day three or four men never come back and he sits back there doing business. . . . I'm going out on a mission in a few minutes. They'll probably report me missing. If they do, I want you to know that you musn't wait for me. I tell you, Ann, . . . I could kill him.

The climax occurs when Joe offers to surrender himself to justice. Kate, however, argues with him: "Larry was your son . . . he'd never tell you to do this"; to which Joe replies: "I think to him they were all my sons. And I guess they were." While Joe is inside the house, Chris tells Kate:

> Once and for all you can know there's a universe of people outside and you're responsible to it, and unless you know that, you threw away your son because that's why he died.

Immediately "a shot is heard in the house." Joe has put a bullet in his head— for Larry has evidently shown Joe that there is "something bigger" than the "family." The play concludes with Chris "almost crying," but with Kate telling him: "Don't take it on yourself. . . . Live!"

Although the structure of All My Sons is tight, it remains open to a number of serious criticisms. My summary of the introduction in act 1 focuses on essential items only and thus fails to reveal the repetition and inconsequential byplay contained in the first sixteen pages of the text. Miller would have it that every step in All My Sons was carefully calculated. We need not necessarily accept this view. The critic who wrote the introduction in 1957 was not the dramatist who wrote the play in 1947. Granting, for the sake of argument, that every move in the play was carefully plotted, one might question whether contrast, which is indeed a powerful dramatic device, could not have been established in a more economical manner, whether a relatively static and lengthy introduction threatening "boredom" was absolutely essential. A more cautious approach might suggest that Miller, in his second full-length play, had not as yet thoroughly mastered certain difficult problems of craft—chiefly, as Miller himself acknowledges, "the biggest single dramatic problem, namely, how to dramatize what has gone before" (introduction to CP).

In addition, Miller seems guilty of having made his dramatic problem easy for himself at the turning point of the play. A "slip of the tongue" is certainly possible, but in the context of the play, is it not made to seem fortuitous? And is it not precisely the fortuitous nature of events that the form of the play is at pains to deny? According to Miller: "The structure of the play is designed to bring a man into the direct path of the consequences he has wrought"; and: "The fortress which *All My Sons* lays siege to is the fortress of unrelatedness" (introduction to *CP*). How is Kate's "slip of the tongue" related to the events of the play? Not only by intention, but through the achieved tightness of structure, Miller forces the reader to question the logic of his play. The most influential interpretation of verbal "slips" in our time is, of course, the Freudian one. Miller, however, provides no evidence in the play for such an interpretation; in fact, there is no explanation given for Kate's "slip"—it must simply be attributed to chance. In dramatic terms, then, the "slip" is not made plausible. When one considers the events that immediately follow upon Kate's blunder, one is inclined to feel that Miller has not faced the dramatic task in a forthright manner.

The arbitrary nature of the action continues in act 3. Aside from the crude foreshadowing device quoted in my summary, Joe Keller shows no evidence of being a potential suicide. As a description of his character will reveal shortly, Joe is lacking in inner conflict; but if modern psychology has taught us anything, it is that none of us—least of all a suicide—is lacking in inner conflict. Kate, it should be noted, is made to threaten suicide in act 1; she says: "if [Larry's] not coming back, then I'll kill myself!" This, like Joe's threat in act 3 looks like foreshadowing. It is beside the point to say that it is in character for Kate to choose life over death. Perhaps, one might argue, Miller intends that Kate's refusal to kill herself reflects freedom in the world of his play; it demonstrates that Joe is not being jerked about arbitrarily by the author, that Joe wills his own destruction. Whatever the rationale behind the strategy, however, it seems to make for confusion rather than complexity, for it tends to weaken Joe's motivation instead of making it appear freely chosen. The question arises: Why *must* Joe kill himself? (One critic has speculated why Joe is strong enough to bear the guilt of his first act but not strong enough to shoulder the second guilt.) One is forced to conclude that Joe Keller kills himself because his suicide is an effective way to drive home the thesis.

The appearance of the letter in act 3 is the most censured device in the play. Only Dennis Welland defends it; he argues that the device is credible, economical, and dramatic. This is a valiant critical defense, but no more convincing, finally, than the play itself. As Kate brought about the turning point, Larry—a character never seen on stage—prepares the climax. The focus, it seems, should be on Joe, not Kate, or Larry, or even Chris. The audience should be made to see—should have been made to see from the first—the slow stages of Joe's movement toward self-destruction. This is why the leisurely introduction is blameworthy. Twenty-four hours is a short time in which to propel a man from "placidity" to a "rage of conscience." The letter itself might very well be "credible" and "economical"; this, however, is not enough. It is, for one thing, a stock device suggesting the "well-made play." Most critics, including the present one, are inclined to feel that the letter is not dramatically convincing. Contrivance also suggests itself in the stagy juxtaposition of Chris's indictment of his parents and the resounding report that immediately follows signalizing the end of Joe Keller's existence. This too is an "economical" and "dramatic" way to drive home the thesis.

The question has been raised about who the protagonist is, structurally, in *All My Sons*. According to one critic, Miller never focuses clearly on Joe Keller; although Joe is central thematically, Chris appears to receive equal attention. According to a second critic, the interest shifts from the protagonist to the antagonist. Some facts are in order. Out of a total number of sixty-eight pages of text, Joe is present on about forty-five pages; Chris is present on about forty-nine pages. Out of a total number of sixty-two scenes, Joe appears in forty-four and Chris in forty-two. A check of speaking lines would reveal the same fairly equal distribution of parts between Joe and Chris. Quantitatively, then, there is a basis for asking who is the protagonist in *Sons*. Qualitatively, analysis seems to suggest that Chris, not Joe, is the most active character in the play. Until the final moments of the last act, Joe is relatively passive. Chris, however, forces the conflict from beginning to end. It is Chris who invites Ann to visit the Keller house; Chris who wants to remove the fiction of Larry's return; Chris who challenges Kate's obsession; Chris who calls Joe to defend his acts; Chris who demands that Joe atone for his crime against humanity. Although Joe carries the burden of the theme, then, Chris is the driving force within the structure. This dichotomy, I believe, damages the play. Not all plays, of course, have an active protagonist (which seems like a contradiction in terms); *Othello* springs quickly to mind. One hesitates to generalize here, for each play must be viewed on its own merits. In *All My Sons,* the shift in emphasis would seem unhappy because Joe's movement toward suicide should be made credible, and, if that movement is to be made credible, the focus should be almost wholly on Joe. It is not that some dramatic "law" demands that Joe seal his own fate. It is that by the logic of *this* play, *All My Sons,* that Joe Keller must convincingly advance to his final gesture as a dramatic character.

This raises, finally, several minor questions of probability. One critic has questioned the appearance of George in act 2. George had not visited his father since the latter was sentenced to jail. Over three years had passed without George sending his father a Christmas card. Why, then, did George suddenly visit his father? George tells Ann: "I wanted to . . . tell him you were going to be married. It seemed impossible not to tell him." One might also consider the engagement of Chris and Ann. When Joe asks "why it has to be Annie," Chris says: "Because it is." Joe, baffled, points out that it is "five years" since Chris has seen Ann, but Chris says:

> I can't help it. I know her best. I was brought up next door to her. These years when I think of someone for my wife, I think of Annie. What do you want, a diagram?

Ann admits that she almost "got married two years ago," but that Chris started writing to her then and she had "felt something"—in fact, she had "felt something" ever since. She did not write, however, because: "I was waiting for you, Chris. Till then you never wrote. And when you did, what did you say? You sure can be ambiguous, you know." The reader suspects that Chris's "ambiguity" stems from his author's desire to save Ann for a crucial moment in the lives of his other characters. There is, in short, too much contrivance here. Why, after ignoring his father for three years, did George suddenly find it "impossible" not to inform the man of Ann's approaching marriage? Why this sudden necessity for respect? One might feel that there is no adequate reason here—except that Miller simply wanted George for the second act. Similarly, the romance between Chris and Ann does not encourage close scrutiny. There is something vague, even a little "mystical," about the coming together of the two lovers that suggests love less than manipulation. These are minor matters, however, and need not be overemphasized—they merely underline more important structural defects.

Ironically Miller, who had intended to write a play that would be "as untheatrical as possible," that would be distinguished by its "artlessness," actually produced the apotheosis of the theatrical and the artful—in other words, a "well-made play." And as William Archer says: "The trouble with the well-made play is that it is almost always . . . ill-made."

Are the characters in *All My Sons* "ill-made," too? Miller, in his opening stage directions, describes Joe Keller in this manner:

*Keller is nearing sixty. A heavy man of stolid mind and build, a business man these many years, but with the imprint of the machine-shop worker and boss still upon him. When he reads, when he speaks, when he listens, it is with the terrible concentration of the uneducated man for whom there is wonder in many commonly known things, a man whose judgments must be dredged out of experience and a peasant-like common sense. A man among men.*

It has been said that there is more "social density" in *All My Sons* than in Miller's previous play. One function of dialogue is to reveal character; it should throw light on the character's past, present, and future. If we examine *All My Sons,* do we find language projecting a dense, complex social world—what, specifically, do we learn about Joe Keller? In act 3, Joe says:

I should've put [Chris] out when he was ten like I was put out, and make him earn his keep. Then he'd know how a buck is made in this world.

This, plus other remarks in the play, indicates that Joe went to work at an early age, that he worked hard, that he had no education, that society in the past fifty years has grown increasingly specialized and complex, and that Joe is somewhat baffled by the changes. Joe is a product of a business society; his ideal is General Motors. Joe's every move, even to shipping defective airplane parts, seems inspired by business values:

I'm in business . . . a hundred and twenty cracked, you're out of business . . . they close you up . . . you lay forty years into a business and they knock you out in five minutes, what could I do, let them take forty years, let them take my life away?

Joe can be cynical about the "big ones": "a little man makes a mistake and they hang him by the thumbs; the big ones become ambassadors." He can, however, also grow vehement:

Did they ship a gun or a truck outa Detroit before they got their price? Is that clean? It's dollars and cents, nickels and dimes; war and peace . . . what's clean?

This completes Joe's social dimension.

Psychologically, Joe is depicted as a humble man; he repeatedly scores his own ignorance. His sense of humor is described by Chris: "George Bernard Shaw as an elephant." Joe knows how to be "practical" in a ruthless society: "I ignore," says Joe, "what I gotta ignore." He boasts about his "guts" in braving the neighbors after his trial. He seems open and straight-forward, but he is capable of deceit and deception; he says: "I never believed in crucifying people"—when he has in fact crucified his best friend, Ann's father. And, finally, Joe is a "family man":

> There's nothin' [Chris] could do that I wouldn't forgive. Because he's my son. Because I'm his father and he's my son.

This is Miller's description of Chris:

> *He is thirty-two; like his father, solidly built, a listener. A man capable of immense affection and loyalty.*

Does dialogue reveal much about Chris's background and social attitudes? Chris says that the "business doesn't inspire me"; he explains:

> I like it an hour a day. If I have to grub for money all day long at least at evening I want it beautiful. I want a family, I want some kids, I want to build something I can give myself to.

Before the first act is over, however, Chris tells Ann: "I'm going to make a fortune for you!" According to Chris, America is a "zoo." In combat, however, it was, says Chris, different:

> They didn't die; they killed themselves for each other. . . . And I got an idea—watching them go down. . . . A kind of—re-sponsibility. Man for man. . . . And then I came home and it was incredible . . . the whole thing to them was a kind of a—bus accident. I went to work with Dad, and that rat-race again.

Psychologically, Chris has many traits. Jim says that Chris "likes every-body." Chris shows that he is not Christ, however, for he cannot forgive everything, he cannot forgive what he regards as unforgivable, namely, the crime that has sent Ann's father to prison. Nevertheless, Chris is longsuf-fering: "Every time I reach out for something I want," he says, "I have to pull back because other people will suffer." Yet Chris is determined to find happiness. He admits to being "old-fashioned"—he "loves his parents." When evidence of Joe's guilt is manifest, however, Chris finally demands that his parent be punished. Chris has "no imagination"; he admits to being "ignorant." He also confesses to being "not fast with women." As has been said, Chris has a sense of guilt; the war, he says: "seemed to make suckers out of a lot of guys. I felt wrong to be alive, to open the bank-book, to drive the new car." The dialogue of other characters casts additional light on Chris. Says Joe: "Everything bothers [Chris]. You make a deal, overcharge two cents, and his hair falls out." Sue, a neighbor, says: "If Chris wants people to put on the hair shirt let him take off his broadcloth." Says Jim, Sue's husband: "I always had the feeling that in the back of his head, Chris . . . almost knew [about Joe]"—but Jim adds: "Chris would never know how to live with a thing like that. It takes a certain talent—for lying." Chris himself says: "I'm yellow . . . because I suspected my father and I did nothing."

In his stage directions, Miller says that Kate "is in her early fifties, a women of uncontrolled inspirations and an overwhelming capacity for love." In the play itself, Kate criticizes Larry, Chris, and George: "You had big principles, Eagle Scouts the three of you." George, who lost his girl, Lydia, to a 4F, Frank, is told: "While you were getting mad about Fascism, Frank was getting into [Lydia's] bed." The ultimate wisdom is: "look after yourself." Kate cares little if Chris's "idealism" dies—the important thing is that he return to the family. When Kate meets George, Miller says: "her pity, open and unabashed, reaches into him"; and Kate says: "it breaks my heart to see what happened to all the children." Kate calls herself "stupid." Perhaps that is why she is scornful of intellect, for she informs Chris and George that they "*think* too much." Kate tells Ann: "Listen to your heart. Only your heart." Kate is also fond of omens: "[Ann] goes to sleep in [Larry's] room," she says, "and his memorial breaks in pieces." Trusting in Frank's star-book, she can say:

> Certain things have to be, and certain things can never be. . . .
> That's why there's God. Otherwise anything could happen. But
> there's God, so certain things can never happen.

Perhaps the most trenchant remark concerning Kate is made by Jim, when he says that Kate has "a certain talent—for lying." Her final word— "Live"—is in character, for Kate has revealed her ability to put unpleasant facts out of mind and "live" all through the play; in this, lies Kate Keller's strength . . . and her weakness.

Physically, none of Miller's characters is individualized in a striking way. Perhaps this is not a serious failing, however, in a form where there are actors to impersonate the playwright's creations. Certainly the stage directions characterize Joe sharply enough, and, as pointed out earlier, Miller reveals in action (to the point of "boredom"?) the features of Joe described in the directions. Although certain facts are related about Joe's background and social attitudes through dialogue, much else is also left blank. We learn nothing about Joe's parents, nothing about his childhood thoughts and feelings (a time, according to moralists and psychologists, when one's character is more or less molded for life), nothing about where Joe came from, nothing, save "the outskirts of an American town," about where he is at present. For a "realistic" play, the dialogue, then, is not wholly satisfactory. Psychologically, Joe has a number of traits; he is not presented under a single aspect. Nevertheless, he remains unsuitable for his specific role. More than an accumulation of traits are required here—the need is for contradictory traits that will directly influence the course of action. Joe Keller lacks these traits.

Dialogue similarly fails to reveal much, if anything, about Chris's childhood, boyhood, or young manhood. We learn only that Ann's family were neighbors to the Kellers while the children werc growing. Chris, however, remains a more complex character than Joe. Chris, for example, is in conflict between the "love ethic" and the "business ethic," but Joe, presumably, feels no such conflict. Chris is also torn between loyalty to Ann and loyalty to his mother; between suspicion of Joe and the need to conceal his doubts from himself. If Joe is easier to believe in than his idealistic son, it is because Joe's philosophy seems to rise up palpably from the concrete and visible action on stage; but Chris must reach back to the past for an actualization of his philosophy (as Miller must reach back into the past for an unseen character to untie the knot). What we get is a *summary* of Chris's development rather than a *dramatic experience* of the thing itself. Consequently, Chris's "ideals" risk sounding too abstract—particularly when Chris, like Joe, yearns for family life and fortune, too. The fact that dialogue fails to illuminate Chris's background likewise militates against our belief in his values. Perhaps Miller is counting on a stock response here. Why should Chris differ from Joe and Kate? What specific factors account for the difference? The war experience does not seem entirely satisfactory as an explanation. Not all the fighting men were so "responsible"; not all the civilians regarded the war as a "bus accident." There is a danger of sentimentality here, the tendency to dichotomize humanity into "good guys" and "bad guys"—in short, a melodramatic vision. Lacking social depth, then, Chris often seems to step out of character to deliver a speech. Like other aspects of the play, the language is frequently too "neat," too obviously didactic.

At first sight, Kate Keller seems complex. A closer view, however, suggests that there is perhaps confusion interlaced with complexity in her characterization. It is Miller's attitude, as reflected in his stage directions, that are disconcerting. Miller says Kate has "uncontrolled inspirations"— but after threatening to kill herself, Kate manages to control her "inspiration." Miller says that Kate has an "overwhelming capacity for love"—

but the play shows that her love has strict limits; like Joe's love, it has a "forty-foot front." Miller says that Kate feels pity for George—but the play shows that Kate, as much as Joe, destroyed George's family. This is not a problem in the theater; for an audience, Kate is a self-deceived woman; but for a reader, there is something incongruous in Miller's conception of Kate. Not satisfactory for either audience or reader, however, is the fact that Kate's dialogue fails to reveal anything at all about her background or development.

Only Chris really grows in the play. Joe is made to grow—and his "jump" is unconvincing. Kate is static. She has experienced some unpleasant events, but there is no indication that she has altered any of her basic attitudes. In act 1, Chris feels guilty and vaguely suspects Joe; in act 2, he learns the truth about Joe, but cannot immediately demand Joe's expiation— hence, his sense of guilt *increases;* but in act 3, Larry's suicide reveals the course that Chris must take, and when the play ends, Chris is presumably free from his sense of guilt and able to enjoy life again. Although the letter device tends to weaken Chris's development too, his movement as a whole seems relatively steady and credible. There has also been preparation for his final action.

None of the minor characters requires detailed discussion. All of them are "flat"; all of them are static. A few of them, such as Bert, Lydia, and Frank, seem superfluous in terms of action. Whether all of them are necessary to the development of the theme will be taken up below. Contrast is not very diverse here; Joe, Kate, Sue, and, to a lesser degree, Frank, are played off against Chris, Ann, George, and Jim. The contrast is a simple one—between those who have "ideals" and those who have no "ideals," or, at least, very limited ones. The minor characters are stock figures: Jim is the "country doctor"; Sue is the "shrew"; George is the "avenger." Frank, unlike the other minor figures, has an interesting psychology, but if you hold that a play should have no spare parts, a case could be made for Frank being unnecessary. Lydia and Bert have no discernible substance. Ann, of course, is the most disappointing character among the minor roles simply because of her position in the plot. A close reading of the text will yield next to nothing about Ann's background, traits, or social attitude. But perhaps these characters can be discussed with more profit in relation to the theme of the play.

In his [1957] introduction, Miller says:

> In its earlier versions the mother . . . was in a dominating po-
> sition . . . her astrological beliefs were given great prominence

. . . because I sought in every sphere to give body and life to connection. But as the play progressed the conflict between Joe and . . . Chris pressed astrology to the wall until its mysticism gave way to psychology. There was also the impulse to regard the mystical with suspicion, since it had, in the past, given me only turgid works that could never develop a true climax based upon revealed psychological truths. . . . [Kate's] obsession now had to be opened up to reveal its core of self-interest.

The key speech of Kate appears near the end of act 2. Here, the "astrological" and the "psychological" meet. Whereas Joe blames the "system," Kate shifts responsibility to "God." The action of the play, however, denies that responsibility can be shifted in this fashion. Kate's "core of self-interest" is also revealed—she believes what she wants to believe. It was noted earlier that for Kate the "heart," not the "head," is the trustworthy part of the anatomy. The play itself, once more, affirms the opposite belief. Chris listens to his "heart" when he hesitates to deliver Joe to justice, but Larry uses his "head," his suicide being a vote for "responsibility" beyond blood ties. Joe and Kate have not been able to identify Larry and Chris with other young men. We are given to understand that Larry never flew a P-40; when Joe states this as a fact, nobody contradicts him. When Ann asks: "how do you know Larry wasn't one of them?" (Ann knows the truth, of course, but she is trying to make a point here, namely, that the Kellers should not morally dissociate the crime from Larry's death.) Kate replies: "As long as you're here, Annie, I want to ask you never to say that again." This line looks forward to Kate's key speech already quoted. There is a problem here, however, that will be analyzed in a moment.

Do the minor characters have significant thematic relevance? Sue says: "Chris makes people want to be better than it's possible to be," which remark links up with Joe's statement: "Chris, a man can't be Jesus in this world!" The play "refutes" both. Frank ("that big dope," as Kate puts it, "who never reads anything but Andy Gump") would seem to lie somewhere between the two contrasting camps mentioned previously. George says: "When I was studying [law] in the hospital it seemed sensible, but outside there doesn't seem to be much of a law." Jim says: "I can't find myself; it's even hard sometimes to remember the kind of man I wanted to be." Ann's commitment is clear from the fact that her "ideals" prevent her from forgiving her father for his crime.

A close study of the crisis and climax of act 3 shows clearly that Joe is not, as one critic has asserted, exonerated; otherwise, why does Miller laboriously introduce the letter and why does Joe, as a consequence, destroy himself? No, one does not necessarily accuse Miller of intellectual confusion here; it is Joe who rationalizes and Chris who, for a time, hesitates and seems to accept the rationalization. Nevertheless, one feels that, in spite of the ending, Miller is also blaming the system. Miller does not seem to say, though, that the system determines man (how could he, in view of the ending?); he suggests, rather, that the system has a strong influence on man. Is this, in the light of sociological data, an unreasonable attitude? Psychologically, it is entirely credible that a son might hesitate for a time to send his own father to prison. (Whether knowingly to withhold shipments of war supplies until a price is fixed, while the lives of fighting men depend on those supplies, is *morally* poles apart from what Joe perpetrated remains a nice point for an ethical philosopher or moral theologian to ponder.) Miller might be open to the charge of not sufficiently distinguishing moral from legal guilt, but in view of what has been said, it would be difficult to make the charge hold—considering the situation of the characters and the ending of the play.

In the discussion of character it was suggested that Kate seemed somewhat confusing as a creation, at least as she appears in the stage directions. It is possible that in the course of his numerous revisions of the play, Miller lost his clear focus on Kate. The question arises, why would Kate connect Joe's crime with Larry's death (and we must believe that Kate knows that Larry never flew a P-40) if she had not, from the start, made the logical transition from "my son, Larry" to "why, they are all my sons"? Joe made this transition ("jump") only when faced with the fact of Larry's suicide—but how did Kate arrive at this state of consciousness? Whatever one's own epistemology, within the context of the play—that is, in the projected polar opposites of "heart" and "head"—it is the "heart" that is suspect, the "head" that is noble. Kate's "heart," then, appears to arrive at a truth that presumably only the "head" can know. Kate is at the core of the plot; her refusal to relinquish her obsession is a source of conflict in the play; her "slip of the tongue" brings about the turning point in the action; and her inflexibility drives Ann into revealing Larry's letter, thus forcing the play to its climax and conclusion. Thematically, however, Kate adds nothing to Joe's characterization, nothing to the basic thrust of the play—in fact, as has been suggested, Kate tends to confuse rather than project the theme.

None of the minor characters seems absolutely essential to the theme. Frank, for example, appears unnecessary because whatever he might contribute to the meaning of the play is already inherent in Kate's role—one stargazer would seem sufficient. It might also be noted that the use of the stars is a crude way to focus the theme; it too overtly suggests "fate in the stars." Equally unfortunate is the too obvious play on Chris as "Christ." Only Ann and George are really integrated with the action. The others are there, no doubt, because Miller felt that their presence added complexity and social extension to the play. They add, in fact, no complexity. Structurally, they delay the point of attack, and that delay has repercussions on the credibility of Joe's development. Thematically, it is questionable whether they succeed in making the play more "significant." Where would one draw the line here? Is the formula: the more characters, the more extension and significance? It would not seem to be a mere matter of numbers. Economy demands that no character is strictly necessary who does not contribute something vital to action or theme. A more liberal view would leave room for a certain amount of "excess baggage" here— but Miller, it seems, has been rather too liberal on this score. In *Ghosts* (a play that many consider Ibsen's masterpiece), there are only five characters—half the number of *All My Sons*—yet Ibsen manages to project a complex social vision.

It has been asserted that *All My Sons* is actually a vote for the family instead of loyalty to the state ("something bigger" than the "family"), for, so the argument goes, Miller does not make clear whether the soldiers under Chris were devoted to an abstract ideal or merely attached to the group—if the latter, it is simply the family in disguise. Although Miller tends to idealize the American soldier, the abstract ideal in the play *is* precisely loyalty to one another, which might be described as a "family" loyalty, but obviously the "family" here extends beyond the narrow limits of one's immediate blood ties. It is an incomplete "family" loyalty only in the sense that it does not include the enemy.

I have suggested that *All My Sons* is a thesis play. Miller says: "I think now that the straight-forwardness of the . . . form was in some part due to the relatively sharp definition of the social aspects of the problem it dealt with" (introduction to *CP*). That the play is more complex than most critics, perhaps even including Miller, have allowed is certainly true. Whether it is complex enough, however, to weather the charge of thesis drama is another matter. Although Joe Keller and the other characters are not depicted as merely pawns of social forces, they *are* pawns of theatrical contrivance, a point which has been sufficiently discussed above. As for the "idea" itself, it would appear to be too explicitly insisted upon, too sermonic in deliverance, and, because sermons tend to oversimplify experience (even the laudable Sermon on the Mount has required volumes of exegesis), Miller seems guilty of ignoring the complexity of experience and the intractability of the human animal.

# $A$ll My Sons and the Larger Context

## Barry Gross

Arthur Miller has always maintained that his plays have not been immediately understood, that *After the Fall* was not about Marilyn Monroe and
*Incident at Vichy* was not about anti–Semitism, that *A View from the Bridge*
was not about longshoremen and *The Crucible* was not about McCarthyism,
that *Death of a Salesman* was not about the business world and *All My Sons*
was not about war-profiteering. What, then, twenty-five years later, is *All
My Sons* about?

In 1947 the generation gap was not the cliché it has since become and
*All My Sons* is certainly, on one level, about that. Joe Keller is almost twice
his son Chris's age. He is an "uneducated man for whom there is still
wonder in many commonly known things," for instance, that new books
are published every week or that a man can earn "a living out of . . . old
dictionaries." He is the product of a vanished America, of a time when
"either you were a lawyer, or a doctor, or you worked in a shop," a time
of limited possibilities for someone "put . . . out at ten" to "earn his keep,"
for someone who learned English in "one year of night-school" and still
does not know what "roué" means or that it is French, still says "brooch"
when he means "broach."

We can only guess at Joe Keller's history because the kind of play
Miller had in mind would, of necessity, exclude it. *All My Sons* was to be
a "jurisprudence," and, as Miller says in the introduction to *Collected Plays,*

From *Modern Drama* 18, no. 1 (March 1975). © 1975 by the University of Toronto,
Graduate Centre for the Study of Drama.

> When a criminal is arraigned . . . it is the prosecutor's job to
> symbolize his behavior for the jury so that the man's entire life
> can be characterized in one way and not in another. The pros-
> ecutor does not mention the accused as a dog lover, a good
> husband and father, a sufferer from eczema, or a man with a
> habit of chewing tobacco on the left and not the right side of
> his mouth.

Well and good: Miller is entitled to establish the design for his own work and to be judged according to the terms he proposes. But the jury is also entitled to hear the defense, indeed must hear it if it is to reach a fair verdict, and Joe Keller's unrevealed history *is* his defense. "Where do you live, where do you come from?" Chris asks him. "Don't you have a country? Don't you live in the world? What the hell are you?" The answers lie buried in Joe Keller's past.

Is he an immigrant? The son of an immigrant? If he had to learn English in night-school, does that mean he grew up speaking German? Yiddish? These are not irrelevant questions if Joe Keller's crime is to be understood in human, rather than aberrational, terms, and it is clearly an important part of Miller's design that Keller's crime be seen as a profoundly human one. There are logical answers to Chris's questions; that Chris cannot imagine them is both result and proof of the generation gap that inevitably separates father and son. The gap can be defined by their differing percep-tions of and attitudes toward the idea and the reality of community. Joe Keller is guilty of an antisocial crime not out of intent but out of ignorance; his is a crime of omission, not of commission. For him there is no society, and there never has been one. It is not simply that Joe's "mind can see" only "as far as . . . the business" or that for Joe "the business" is "the world." Actually, he does not see as far as that and for him the world is smaller. Where does he live? He lives at home. Does he live in the world? No. Does he have a country? No. What the hell is he? Provider, bread-winner, husband and father. His world is bounded by the picket fence that encloses the suburban back yard in which the play takes place, his com-mitments and allegiances do not extend beyond its boundaries. He is an engaged man, but not to man or to men, only to his family, more precisely to his sons, not all the sons of the title but the two sons he has fathered.

"In my day," Joe Keller says wistfully, "when you had a son it was an honor." What else "did [he] work for?" That is not an excuse but it is an explanation. It is not that Joe Keller cannot distinguish between right and wrong, it is that his understanding of what is right and what is wrong has been ineluctably determined by the only reality he has ever known. When he advises Ann not to hate her father he begs her to "see it human," and if we fail to see Joe Keller human then we relegate him to that dark otherworld where only monsters dwell, safely removed from the world in which we think we live so we do not have to identify with it or admit our own compliance in it. What is right in Joe Keller's ethos—and it *is* an ethos—is the familial obligation, the father's duty to create something for his son. He is not proud of being a self-made man or of his material success, he is proud that he has made something for his son. There is no zealot like a convert and there is probably no more devoted parent than a neglected or an abandoned child. We know that Willy Loman was abandoned by his father when he was an infant, and that goes far to explain his passionate involvement in his sons' lives. If Joe's father turned him out at age ten, it is not surprising that his first article of faith should be "a father is a father and a son is a son." Impossible as it may be for Chris to understand or appreciate the fact, Joe was keeping that faith when he shipped out the faulty plane parts: "I did it for you, it was a chance and I took it for you. I'm sixty-one years old, when would I have another chance to make something for you? . . . For you, a business for you!" Misguided, yes; malevolent, no, no more so, in intent, than Willy Loman's suicide, Willy's refusal to die empty-handed, Willy's commitment to the paternal obligation as he understands it, Willy's need to express his love for his son in the only way he knows how. Joe "didn't want [the money] that way" any more than Willy wanted it the way he chose, but he had "a family" and for Joe "nothin' is bigger . . . than the family": "There's nothin' he could do that I wouldn't forgive. Because he's my son. Because I'm his father and he's my son. . . . Nothin's bigger than that. . . . I'm his father and he's my son." There is literally no other frame of reference. It is not only that "a man can't be a Jesus in this world," it is that, to Joe, Jesus is irrelevant. Jesus was never a father.

As a change of heart and a change of mind the denouement is, thus, unconvincing. Joe promises to "put a bullet in [his] head . . . if there's something bigger" than family, he reads Larry's letter, agrees that "they were . . . all [his] sons," and shoots himself. Joe Keller has not overthrown sixty years of thinking and feeling in a minute. Like Willy Loman, he goes to his death deluded, dies in the name of his delusion, dies a believer. He knows only that his sons think there is something bigger than family, that he has shamed them, one to the point of suicide, that his sons for whom he has lived consider him an animal and do not want to live in the same world with him. Joe's suicide is less a moral judgment than an act of love.

In effect, Joe kills himself so that Chris need not kill *him*self—Chris: "What must I do?"—and because Chris tells him to—Chris: "Now you tell me what you must do." Joe commits his second antisocial crime in the name of the same love that motivated the first.

For Joe Keller there is no conflict beyond the fact that time has passed and values have, at least according to his sons, changed. The conflict in the play is Chris Keller's, not so much between him and his father, or between his generation's and his father's, but within his own generation, within himself. Chris's is the conflict between who and what he is and who and what he wants to be, or thinks he ought to be. He wants to be, or thinks he ought to be, different from his father. Watching his comrades die for each other and for him, he has become aware of "a kind of—responsibility, man to man." Upon returning from the war, he had thought "to bring that on to the earth again like some kind of a monument and everyone would feel it standing there, behind him, and it would make a difference to him." He knows that if he is alive at all "to open the bank-book, to drive the new car, to see the new refrigerator," it is because "of the love a man can have for a man." Yet when Chris returns home he finds "no meaning in it here," finds that "nobody . . . changed at all."

So Chris knows things his father cannot know, and yet he remains his father's son. He will spend his life in a business that "doesn't inspire" him for more than "an hour a day," he will "grub for money all day long," if it can be "beautiful" when he comes home in the evening. The only monument he can think to build is precisely the one his father has constructed: "I want a family, I want some kids, I want to build something I can give myself to. . . . Oh, Annie, Annie, I'm going to make a fortune for you!" In this light, it is not fair for Chris to make other people feel guilty for their "compromises" or for their inability or unwillingness "to be better than it's possible to be." Chris makes no visible efforts to be better than it is possible to be, or even to be as good as it is possible to be. Sue's branding of Chris as hypocrite—"if Chris wants people to put on the hair shirt let him take off his broadcloth"—is valid. His shame and guilt are meaningless because they do not lead to action. Society's case against Chris Keller is stronger than its case against Joe Keller because Chris knows better. His tendency is to embroider what he obviously thinks of as an unacceptable reality—Ann: "As soon as you get to know somebody you find a distinction for them"—rather than to attempt to transform that reality into something different, something better.

Chris's self-proclaimed love for his parents is also suspect. "You're the only one I know who loves his parents," Ann exclaims, to which he replies with some self-congratulation, "I know. It went out of style, didn't it?" He thinks his father is "a great guy," he promises his mother he will "protect" them against George's attacks—but Chris's devotion to his father is based on his assumption that "the man is innocent." He could not love a guilty father, not out of moral fastidiousness but out of self-love. If, as George says, Chris has lied to himself about his father's guilt, it is more to deny what he himself is than what his father is. When Biff Loman stumbles and weeps when he discovers at age seventeen that his father is not the god he thought him, we understand that an adolescent has made a painful but inevitable discovery. When Chris Keller, who has been "a killer" in the war, does the same thing at thirty-two, we must conclude that he is responding to some private drama unwinding inside him rather than to the revelation of his father's guilt. Even his mother is surprised that it is "such a shock" to him; she "always had a feeling that in the back of his head . . . Chris almost knew." Jim insists that Chris could not have known because he "would never know how to live with a thing like that," but Jim idolizes Chris, though we never see why, and his testimony is not reliable. Chris has not allowed himself to admit what he knew *because* he would not know how to live with it. Chris will come back, Jim tells Kate, he will make the necessary compromise; he has gone off so he can "be alone to watch . . . the star of [his] honesty . . . go out." The star Chris has gone out to watch flicker and die is not the star of his honesty but the star of his image of himself as honest, not the fact of his innocence but the lie of his innocence which he has persisted in believing. It is not that he *will* compromise himself, it is that he *has* compromised himself, and now he can no longer deny it.

When Chris returns from his vigil he admits that he "suspected his father and . . . did nothing about it," less in the name of love of father, we suspect, than of love of self. Like his brother Larry, Chris could not imagine himself such a man's son, he would not be able to "face anybody" or himself. Joe Keller's sin, it would seem, is not so much that he profited from the war or sold faulty plane parts to the government or indirectly caused the deaths of twenty-one men, but that, in revealing himself to be no better "than most men," he "broke his son's heart." For Chris "thought" he *was* "better," that distinction he must assign those he knows: "I never saw you as a man. I saw you as my father. I can't look at you this way. I can't look at myself!" An unwittingly illuminating admission: he cannot look at his father as no better than most *because* he cannot look at himself as no better than most, he has never seen his father as a man because he has not wanted to see himself as one. In act 1 Sue makes a remark about how uncomfortable it is living next door to the Holy Family and now we know what she means: as long as Joe (Jehovah?) is The Father, Chris (Christ?) is surely the son, by definition. What Chris cannot forgive Joe for is that, by his crime, the father has robbed the son of his "distinction." Chris laments that he is "like everyone else now," meaning he is "practical now" like "the cats in the alley" and "the bums who ran away when we were fighting," meaning he is not "human any more." But the converse is true: he is now and finally human *because* he must admit he is like everybody else. If "only the dead ones weren't practical." Chris has always been practical but has never admitted it. Quentin reaches the same conclusion in *After the Fall*: no one who did not die in the concentration camps, he says, can ever be innocent again. As a survivor, Chris will have to learn to live with his "practicality," which is his loss of innocence, which is his humanity.

We do not see this happen. Chris is allowed to have Miller's final words and to point the moral of the play: "It's not enough . . . to be sorry. . . . You can be better! Once and for all you can know there's a universe of people outside and you're responsible to it." Fine words, but their validity is undercut by our knowledge that Chris no more lives in that world outside than his father does, and his father has, at least, always known where he has lived. Similarly, Chris's criticism of America—"This is the land of the great big dogs, you don't love a man here, you eat him. That's the principle; the only one we live by. . . . This is a zoo, a zoo!" — is compromised by his own inability to put the great principle he presumably learned in the war into practice and his own inability to love. However narrowly his values are circumscribed by the family circle, Joe does love, Joe does live by another and better principle, one he is even willing to die for. The gunshot with which Joe ends his life casts Chris's fine words into a silent void because we know that, behind them, Chris is incapable of the commitment and love his father's suicide represents. Not only is Chris incapable of fulfilling his responsibility to the universe of people out there, he is even incapable of assuming his responsibility for the few people in here, in the enclosed back yard: his last words in the play are "Mother, I didn't mean to—." But he did, and that, too, Chris will have to learn to live with.

The Arthur Miller who wrote *All My Sons*, Miller told Josh Greenfield in a 1972 interview for the *New York Times Sunday Magazine*, thought of "writing as legislating, as though the world was to be ordered by the implications in [his] work." He thought then, he says in the introduction to *Collected Plays*, of each member of his audience as "carrying about with him what he thinks is an anxiety, or a hope, or a preoccupation which is his alone and isolates him from mankind," and of the play as the antidote to that condition, as "an experience which widens his awareness of connection," which reveals "him to himself so that he may touch others by virtue of the revelation of his mutuality with them." He thought all serious plays had that function, but especially *All My Sons,* in which he meant to lay "siege" to the specific "fortress of unrelatedness," in which he meant to arraign a particularly heinous antisocial crime, Joe Keller's failure to acknowledge "any viable connection with his world, his universe, or his society." His ultimate goal in the play was to suggest a new order, "the right way to live so that the world is a home and not a battleground or a fog in which disembodied spirits pass each other in an endless twilight."

But it is precisely in Miller's own terms, it is precisely as legislation, that *All My Sons* fails, fails where, oddly enough, *Death of a Salesman,* a far less obviously "legislative" work, succeeds. The similarities between *All My Sons* and *Death of a Salesman* are sufficiently obvious to render their elucidation unnecessary, but something should be said about the basic difference between them. *Death of a Salesman,* Miller says in the *Collected Plays* introduction, grew from "simple" but specific "images":

> From a little frame house on a street of little frame houses, which had once been loud with the noise of growing boys, and then was empty and silent and finally occupied by strangers. Strangers who could not know with what conquistadorial joy Willy and his boys once re-shingled the roof. Now it was quiet in the house, and the wrong people in the beds.
>
> It grew from images of futility—the cavernous Sunday afternoons polishing the car. Where is that car now? And the chamois cloths carefully washed and put up to dry, where are the chamois cloths?
>
> And the endless, convoluted discussions, wonderments, arguments, belittlements, encouragements, fiery resolutions, abdications, returns, partings, voyages out and voyages back, tremendous opportunities and small, squeaking denouements— and all in the kitchen now occupied by strangers who cannot hear what the walls are saying.
>
> The image of aging and so many of your friends already gone and strangers in the seats of the mighty who do not know you or your triumphs or your incredible value.
>
> The image of the son's hard, public eye upon you, no longer swept by your myth, no longer rousable from his separateness,

no longer knowing you have lived for him and have wept for him.

The image of ferocity when love has turned to something else and yet is there, is somewhere in the room if one could only find it.

The image of people turning into strangers who only evaluate one another.

Above all, the image of a need greater than hunger or sex or thirst, a need to leave a thumbprint somewhere on the world.

In short, *Death of a Salesman* is dominated and conditioned by the father's point of view, and *All My Sons* is one of those plays Miller derides in "The Shadow of the Gods" as being dominated by "the viewpoint of the adolescent," one of those predictable plays "in which a young person, usually male, usually sensitive, is driven either to self-destructive revolt or impotency by the insensitivity of his parents, usually the father." As such, *All My Sons* bears less of a resemblance to *Death of a Salesman* than it does to *Cat on a Hot Tin Roof,* or, rather, to Miller's reading of Williams's play:

Essentially it is . . . seen from the viewpoint of the son. He is a lonely young man sensitized to injustice. And his is a world whose human figures partake in various ways of grossness. . . . In contrast, Brick conceives of his friendship with his dead friend as an idealistic, even gallant and valorous and somehow elevated one. . . . He clings to this image as to a banner of purity to flaunt against the world.

For Brick, read Chris; for Brick's dead friend, read Chris's dead comrades-in-arms. But Miller insists that *Cat on a Hot Tin Roof* ultimately fails, not because of the adolescent viewpoint, which "is precious because it is revolutionary and insists upon justice," but because Williams fails "to open up ultimate causes," because the father should have been "forced to the wall in justification of his world" and the son should have been "forced to his wall in justification of his condemning that world," because the father should not have been portrayed as "the source of injustice" but as "its deputy," not as "the final authority" but as "the shadow of the gods." As he told the *Paris Review* interviewers, Williams, in emphasizing "the mendacity of human relations . . . bypasses the issue which the play seems . . . to raise, namely the mendacity in social relations." No play that ignores social relations, Miller argues in "The Family in Modern Drama," can achieve what he considers to be the goal and justification of drama, an "ultimate relevancy to the survival of the race," because, as he insists must be "obvious to any intelligence, . . . the fate of mankind is social."

It is useful to keep Miller's criticisms of *Cat on a Hot Tin Roof* in mind as we turn to a consideration of the failures of *All My Sons*. Most notable is what might be termed its failure in mode, a serious flaw in methodology: Simply and baldly stated, the play is too insistently "realistic"—which is, of course, what Miller meant it to be—to accommodate Chris's fine speeches or to give any weight or resonance to their words. In the narrow and pedestrian setting of the Keller backyard they announce themselves as speeches, in this mundane place the words ring loud and hollow. Miller himself provides the best analysis of this conflict of modes in "The Family in Modern Drama," in which he argues that "the force or pressure that makes for Realism, that even requires it, is the magnetic force of the family relation within the play, and the pressure which evolves in a genuine, unforced way the unrealistic modes is the social relation within the play." The realistic mode is adequate to *All My Sons* as long as the play is dominated by the family relation; it is not adequate to the social relation Miller requires the play to represent, nor does Miller attempt to express that social relation in another, less realistic mode. The problem is clearly illustrated in the case of appropriate stage speech:

> When one is speaking to one's family one uses a certain level of speech, a certain plain diction perhaps, a tone of voice, an inflection, suited to the intimacy of the occasion. But when one faces an audience . . . it seems right and proper for him to reach for the well-turned phrase, even the poetic word, the aphorism, the metaphor.

Chris's speeches fall flat because they violate our sense of suitability, our sense of context. They are made at the wrong time in the wrong place to the wrong people.

What Miller might have done is suggested by his discussion of how other playwrights have handled similar problems. Ibsen solved them by bursting "out of the realistic frame" altogether when he came to write *Peer Gynt,* leaving behind not only "the living room" but "the family context" as well, to allow Peer Gynt to confront "non-familial, openly social relations and forces." *All My Sons* does not burst out of the living room, or, more precisely, the backyard, and yet Miller insists that his characters confront nonfamilial, openly social relations and forces which exist only beyond it. The result is that same tension Miller feels in *The Cocktail Party,* that "sense of . . . being drawn in two opposite directions." In Eliot's play, Miller argues, the tension is created by the language, or, rather, by "the natural unwillingness of our minds to give to the husband-wife relation—a family relation—the prerogatives of the poetic mode," whereas no such problem existed in Eliot's more successful *Murder in the Cathedral* which "had the unquestioned right to the poetic" because its situation was "social, the conflict of a human being with the world." It is, of course, Miller's thematic and philosophic intention to draw us in two opposite directions in *All My Sons,* to dramatize the polar conflict between the familial and the social. But he fails to counter the natural unwillingness of our minds to give to the social relation the prerogatives of the prosaic mode. We grant *All My Sons* the unquestioned right to the prosaic as long as its situation is familial, but if the situation is also to be social, then Miller must extend his play to the poetic, not just in language but also in concept, as, he argues, Thorton Wilder does in *Our Town:*

> The preoccupation of the entire play is . . . the town, the society, and not primarily this particular family—and every stylistic means used is to the end that the family foreground be kept in its place, merely as a foreground for the larger context behind and around it. . . . This larger context . . . is the bridge to the poetic for this play. Cut out the town and you will cut out the poetry.

Miller's preoccupation in *All My Sons* is no less social than Wilder's, but the society never becomes the larger context it is in *Our Town.* In Miller's play the foreground the Keller family occupies looms too large, so large as to obliterate any other context which might or should be behind or around it.

The absence of the larger context does not represent a failure in technique alone—it also represents, and more unaccountably, a failure in content. Miller says in the introduction to *Collected Plays* that *All My Sons* is usually criticized for lack of subtlety, for being too insistently "moral" and too aggressively "straightforward," but I want to argue that, for its stated intentions, the play is not straightforward enough. During an interesting interview with Philip Gelb, published under the title of "Morality and Modern Drama," Miller recalls "a book by Thomas Mann about Moses in which . . . he portrays Moses as being a man bedevilled by the barbaric backwardness of a stubborn people and trying to improve them and raise up their sights," the Ten Commandments being Moses' "way of putting into capsule form what probably the most sensitive parts of the society were wishing would be stated," Moses' attempt to "pinpoint . . . things that were otherwise amorphous and without form." That is no less, Miller would certainly agree, the writer's presumption and his function. In *All My Sons* Miller is not guilty of presuming to teach, or even of presuming to preach, but of not doing it with sufficient force and directness, of not pinpointing with sufficient sharpness Chris's amorphous and formless sentiments. *That* the world should be reordered is not at issue; *how* it should is.

"Where the son stands," Miller says in "The Shadow of the Gods," "is where the world should begin." But this does not happen in *All My Sons* any more than it does in the "adolescent" plays Miller criticizes. It is undeniably true that "the struggle for mastery—for the freedom of manhood . . . as opposed to the servility of childhood—is the struggle not only to overthrow authority but to reconstitute it anew," but by this token Chris has achieved neither mastery nor manhood by the play's end. It might be argued that it is only after the play ends that Chris is equipped to make the world begin, to reconstitute authority anew, that is, only after he learns that his brother killed himself and watches his father do the same thing. If so, that is a high price in human life—to Miller, perhaps because he is not Christian, the highest price imaginable—to rouse Chris Keller to action. And, judging from Chris's past record, one cannot be sure that these two deaths will have that effect. The deaths of his comrades presented him with that opportunity before the play began and he has done nothing to reconstitute authority in their name. If we are to take Chris's stated sentiments about the men who died so that he might live seriously, then he is in the position at the beginning of *All My Sons* that Miller (in the *Sunday Times Magazine* article "Our Guilt for the World's Evil") sees the Jewish psychiatrist in at the end of *Incident at Vichy:* his is "the guilt of surviving his benefactors" and whether he is "a 'good' man for accepting his life in this way, or a 'bad' one, will depend on what he makes of his guilt, of his having survived." By that criterion, Chris Keller is a bad man when *All My Sons* begins and he is no better when the play ends.

Am I arraigning Miller unfairly? Am I asking more of his play than it need do or is supposed to do? Is not Miller entitled to exclude Chris Keller's vision of the future as well as Joe Keller's past in order to pinpoint the particular crime Joe is being prosecuted for? I think not. Our full awareness of that crime and our willingness to convict him of it is based on our belief that a better world is not only preferable but possible, that it not only should be made but could be made. Joe Keller's failure to find a connection with the world is a crime only if there is a world to connect with and only if there is a way to connect with it. Chris's case would be strengthened if, for instance, he expressed himself in the terms in which Miller defines the meaningful rebellions of the sixties generation in "The War Between Young and Old":

> When a man has spent the best years of his life punishing himself with work he hates, telling himself that in his sacrifice lie honor and decency, it is infuriating to confront young people who think it is stupid to waste a life doing hateful work. It is maddening to hear that work ought to be a pleasure, a creative thing rather than a punishment, and that there is no virtue in submission to the waste of one's precious life.

These are, essentially, the terms, if not the immediate causes, of Biff Loman's rebellion. But Chris Keller does not have or propound a theory of work different from his father's: he will waste his precious life doing hateful work as long as he can have it beautiful in the evening when he comes home to wife and kids. As Miller admits in the introduction to *Collected Plays,* Chris does not "propose to liquidate the business built in part on soldiers' blood; he will run it himself, but cleanly." Perhaps; the only line in the play that allows for even this modest hope is Joe's remark that Chris gets upset about a two-cent overcharge.

Chris should not be at such a loss to know how to reconstitute authority anew. If, as he complains, nothing changed at home, and if, as he says, it is a moral imperative for those who have survived to return home to change things, he should know what kind of changes should be made and how they might be accomplished. Chris is, after all, a contemporary of Miller's; he grew up in the depression thirties, he is a member of the generation Miller describes in "The Bored and the Violent," a generation "contemptuous of the given order" which translated its contempt into social action—"joining demonstrations of the unemployed, pouring onto campuses to scream of some injustice by college administrations, and adopting to one degree or another a Socialist ideology." It might be argued that the postwar forties was a different time altogether, that the Socialist ideology was not as attractive as it had been in the thirties. But Miller is his own best argument against such contentions: He certainly did not hesitate to involve himself in causes and programs which promised to alleviate social injustice. As he told the House Committee on Un-American activities, he was not "a dupe" or "a child" but "an adult . . . looking for the world that would be perfect," an honorable and, to Miller's way of thinking, necessary search. As a child of the thirties he knew where to look—to that "old illusion" Miller pays tribute to in *In Russia*

which the great October Revolution raised before the world—
that a government of and by the insulted and injured had finally
risen on the earth, a society which had somehow abolished the
motivations for immorality, the incarnation at long last of the
human community.

Miller translated the Russian idea into American terms in his radio play
*That They May Win,* a modest playlet which achieves in fifteen minutes
the larger context two hours of *All My Sons* fails to approximate and which
suggests the direction *All My Sons* might have—and should have—taken.
A soldier returns from the war to find his wife and child living in a slum
and prices out of control. Like Chris, he was a killer in the war, he is
"proud" that he "killed twenty-eight of the lowest dogs in the world," but
unlike Chris he has learned from his experience: He has learned the efficacy
of united action, and he is appalled by his wife's apparent apathy toward
and helplessness before unfair conditions:

> What's the matter with you? They knock you down; they walk
> all over you; you get up, brush yourself off and say it's workin'
> out great. What do you pay taxes for; what do you vote for?
> . . . What do you do, just go around and let them take the money
> out of your pocket? Doesn't anybody say anything? What're
> they all, dumb? . . . Write to Congress . . . stand on the street
> corner . . . go to the Mayor . . . talk!

True, we are still in the backyard, the living room, the kitchen. But Miller
even tackles and even solves that problem in this play, a contrived borrow-
ing from Pirandello, but a solution nevertheless: A member of the audience
begins to argue with the actors, others argue with him, and finally one
man emerges as spokesman and makes the speech that the actors concede
would have ended the "play" had they been allowed to continue, a speech
much more acceptable coming from him than if "husband" had made it to
"wife":

> You got to *keep* fighting. The people can work it out. . . . You
> don't seem to realize the power we got. . . . Enough people
> together can do anything! . . . Don't it stand to reason in a
> democracy? The big guys have organized to lobby for laws *they*
> want in Washington. What about the people waking up and
> doing the same thing? . . . We the people gotta go into politics.
> . . . You have to go to those Senators and Congressmen you

elected and say, "Listen here, Mister! We're your boss and you have to work for us!"

Idealistic, to be sure, maybe even an illusion. But an ideal and an illusion worthy of and necessary to anyone—Chris or Miller—who believes in the even older ideal, the even greater illusion, that the world can be saved and that the individual can do something about saving it.

# The Action and Its Significance: Miller's Struggle with Dramatic Form

*Orm Överland*

"There are two questions I ask myself over and over when I'm working," Arthur Miller has remarked. "What do I mean? What am I trying to say?" The questions do not cease when a play is completed but continue to trouble him. In the introduction to his *Collected Plays* Miller is constantly asking of each play: "What did I mean? What was I trying to say?" These questions and the playwright's attempts to answer them are directly related to his account of how he planned and wrote his next play.

The process of playwriting is given a peculiar wavelike rhythm in Miller's own story of his efforts to realize his intentions from one play to the other. Troughs of dejection on being exposed to unexpected critical and audience responses to a newly completed play are followed by swells of creativity informed by the dramatist's determination to make himself more clearly understood in the next one. This wavelike rhythm of challenge and response is the underlying structural principle of Miller's introduction to his *Collected Plays*. Behind it one may suspect the workings of a radical distrust of his chosen medium. The present essay will consider some of the effects both of this distrust of the theater as a means of communication and of Miller's theories of dramatic form on his career as a dramatist.

Arthur Miller is not alone in asking what he is trying to say in his plays, nor in being concerned that they may evoke other responses than those the playwright thought he had aimed at. From the early reviews of *Death of a Salesman* critics have observed that a central problem in the

From *Modern Drama* 18, no. 1 (March 1975). © 1975 by the University of Toronto, Graduate Centre for the Study of Drama.

evaluation of Miller's work is a conflict of themes, real or apparent, within each play.

The case for the prosecution has been well put by Eric Bentley:

> Mr. Miller says he is attempting a synthesis of the social and the psychological, and, though one may not see any synthesis, one certainly sees the thesis and the antithesis. In fact, one never knows what a Miller play is about: politics or sex. If *Death of a Salesman* is political, the key scene is the one with the tape recorder; if it's sexual, the key scene is the one in the Boston hotel. You may say of *The Crucible* that it isn't about McCarthy, it's about love in the seventeenth century. And you may say of *A View from the Bridge* that it isn't about informing, it's about incest and homosexuality.

John Mander points to the same conflict in his analysis of *Death of a Salesman* in his *The Writer and Commitment:*

> If we take the "psychological" motivation as primary, the "social" documentation seems gratuitous, if we take the "social" documentation as primary, the "psychological" motivation seems gratuitous. And we have, I am convinced, to choose which kind of motivation must have the priority; we cannot have both at once.

Mr. Mander's own image of this conflict of themes within Arthur Miller's play is the house divided and its two incompatible masters are Freud and Marx.

More sympathetic critics find that the plays successfully embody the author's intentions of dramatizing a synthesis of the two kinds of motivation. Edward Murray, for instance, has made the same observation as have Bentley and Mander, but in his view the difficulty of branding Miller either a "social" or a "psychological" dramatist points to a strength rather than to a flaw in his work: "At his best, Miller has avoided the extremes of clinical psychiatric case studies on the one hand and mere sociological reports on the other. . . . he has indicated . . . how the dramatist might maintain in delicate balance both personal and social motivation."

Miller himself has often spoken of modern drama in general and his own in particular in terms of a split between the private and the social. In the 1956 essay "The Family in Modern Drama," he claims that the various forms of modern drama "express human relationships of a particular kind, each of them suited to express either a primarily familial relation at one extreme, or a primarily social relation at the other." At times he has pointed to his own affinity with one or the other of these two extreme points of view on human relationships, as when he talks of the forties and fifties as "an era of gauze," for which he finds Tennessee Williams mainly responsible: "One of my own feet stands in this stream. It is a cruel, romantic neuroticism, a translation of current life into the war within the self. The personal has triumphed. All conflict tends to be transformed into sexual conflict." More often, as in "The Shadow of the Gods," Miller has seen himself primarily in the social tradition of the thirties. It is in this essay that Miller makes one of his most explicit statements on the need for a synthesis of the two approaches:

> Society is inside of man and man is inside society, and you cannot even create a truthfully drawn psychological entity on the stage until you understand his social relations and their power to make him what he is and to prevent him from being what he is not. The fish is in the water and the water is in the fish.

Such synthesis, however, is fraught with problems which are closely connected with Miller's medium, the theater.

Indeed, for Miller synthesis has largely been a question of dramatic form, and the problem for the playwright has been to create a viable form that could bridge "the deep split between the private life of man and his social life." In addition to his frustration with audience responses and his desire to make himself more clearly understood, part of the momentum behind Miller's search for new and more satisfactory modes of expression after the realistic All My Sons has been the conviction that the realistic mode in drama was an expression of "the family relationship within the play" while "the social relationship within the play" evoked the unrealistic modes.

In retrospect Miller found that the theme of All My Sons (1947) "is the question of actions and consequences," and the play dramatizes this theme in the story of Joe Keller, for whom there was nothing bigger than the family, and his son Chris, for whom "one new thing was made" out of the destruction of the war: "A kind of—responsibility. Man for man." When Miller is slightly dissatisfied with his first successful play, it is because he believes that he had allowed the impact of what he calls one kind of "morality" to "obscure" the other kind "in which the play is primarily interested." These two kinds of "morality" are closely related to the two kinds of "motivation"—psychological and social—that John Mander and other critics have pointed to. The problem may be seen more clearly by observing that the play has two centers of interest. The one, in which Miller claims "the play is primarily interested," is intellectual, the other emotional. The former is mainly expressed through the play's dialogue, the latter is more deeply embedded in the action itself.

Joe Keller gradually emerges as a criminal. He has sold defective cylinder heads to the air force during the war and was thus directly responsible for the deaths of twenty-one pilots. The horror of this deed is further brought home to the audience by the discovery that Keller's elder son was a pilot lost in action. This is what we may call the emotional center of interest, and most of the plot is concerned with this past crime and its consequences for Keller and his family. But it is this emotional center that for Miller obscures the real meaning of the play.

Miller wanted his play to be about "unrelatedness":

> Joe Keller's trouble, in a word, is not that he cannot tell right from wrong but that his cast of mind cannot admit that he, personally, has any viable connection with his world, his universe, or his society. . . . In this sense Joe Keller is a threat to society and in this sense the play is a social play. Its "socialness" does not reside in its having dealt with the crime of selling defective materials to a nation at war—the same crime could easily be the basis of a thriller which would have no place in social dramaturgy. It is that the crime is seen as having roots in a certain relationship of the individual to society, and to a certain indoctrination he embodies, which, if dominant, can mean a jungle existence for all of us no matter how high our buildings soar.

This, then, is the intellectual center of the play. Any good drama needs to engage the intellect as well as the emotions of its audience. Miller's problem is that these two spheres in *All My Sons* are not concentric. When a play has two centers of interest at odds with each other, the emotional one will often, as here, have a more immediate impact on the audience because it is more intimately related to the action of the play. Invariably action takes precedence over the sophistication of dialogue or symbols.

*Death of a Salesman* (1949) may serve as further illustration of the point made about the two centers of interest in *All My Sons*. Bentley wrote that the key scene of the play could be the one in Howard Wagner's office or the one in the hotel room depending on whether the play was "political" or "sexual." There is no doubt, however, as to which scene has the greater impact in the theater. The hotel room scene is carefully prepared for. The constant references to stockings and the growing tension around the repeated queries about what had happened to Biff after he had gone to ask his father's advice in Boston are some of the factors that serve to highlight this scene. A more immediate impression is made on the audience by the mysterious laughter and the glimpse of a strange woman quite early in the first act. The point is, however, that it is primarily on the stage that this scene makes such an overwhelming impact that it tends to overshadow the other scenes that together make up the total image of Willy's plight. If the play is read, if one treats it as one would a novel, balance is restored and a good case may be made for a successful synthesis of "psychological" and "social" motivation as argued, for instance, by Edward Murray.

Miller seems to have become increasingly aware of the difficulty of making a harmonious whole of his vehicle and his theme. His story would have sexual infidelity (consider for instance the prominence this factor must have in any brief retelling of the plot of *Death of a Salesman* or *The Crucible*) or another personal moral failure at its center, while the significance the story held for the author had to do with man's relationship to society, to the outside world. The one kind of "morality" continues to obscure the other. When starting out to write *A View from the Bridge* (1955), Miller had almost despaired of making himself understood in the theater: no "reviews, favorable or not," had mentioned what he had considered the main theme of *The Crucible* (1953). Since he, apparently, could not successfully merge his plots and his intended themes, he arrived at a scheme that on the face of it seems preposterous: he would "separate, openly and without concealment, the action of the next play, *A View from the Bridge,* from its generalized significance."

With such an attitude to the relationship between story and theme or "action" and "significance" there is little wonder that Miller was prone to writing plays where critics felt there was a conflict of themes. For while Miller's imagination generates plots along psychoanalytic lines, his intellect leans towards socioeconomic explanations.

The story was, according to his own account, his starting point for *A View from the Bridge:*

> I had heard its story years before, quite as it appears in the play, and quite as complete. . . . It was written experimentally not only as a form, but as an exercise in interpretation. I found in myself a passionate detachment toward its story as one does toward a spectacle in which one is not engaged but which holds a fascination deriving from its monolithic perfection. If this had happened, and if I could not forget it after so many years, *there*

*must be some meaning in it for me, and I could write what had happened, why it had happened, and to one side, as it were, express as much as I knew of my sense of its meaning for me. Yet I wished to leave the action intact so that the onlooker could seize the right to interpret it entirely for himself and to accept or reject my reading of its significance.*

(my italics)

This decision, Miller explains, led to the creation of "the engaged narrator," the role played by Alfieri in *A View from the Bridge*.

The narrator is hardly an innovation in the history of dramatic literature, especially when seen in relation to the chorus in Greek drama. In our own time widely different playwrights like Thornton Wilder (*Our Town*) and Bertolt Brecht (*The Caucasian Chalk Circle*) have made successful use of the narrator. Such historical antecedents and the widespread use of narrators in modern drama should not be lost sight of when considering this aspect of Arthur Miller's plays. Miller's narrators, however, are closely connected with his reluctance to let his plays speak for themselves. They are born from his long and troubled struggle with dramatic form.

Arthur Miller had tried his hand at fiction as well as drama before he achieved success on Broadway with *All My Sons* in 1947. When he thought of his next play, his aim was to achieve "the density of the novel form in its interchange of viewpoints." Again and again he comments on *Death of a Salesman* in terms of a prose narrative, as when he contrasts its sense of time with that of *All My Sons:* "This time, if I could, I would have *told the whole story* and set forth all the characters in one unbroken speech or even one sentence or a single flash of light. As I look at the play now its form seems the form of a confession, for that is *how it is told*" (my italics). Although this may merely be a manner of speaking, as suggested by his own critique of the movie version where "drama becomes narrative," it does point to an attitude that in certain respects runs counter to drama: the story as something to be *told* as opposed to something to be *shown* or dramatised.

In fact, however, *Death of a Salesman* succeeds precisely because Willy's story is shown on the stage, not told. The possible uncertainty as to motivation does not detract from the intense and unified impact of the drama in the theater. The characters reveal themselves through action and dialogue supported by what Miller has called the play's "structural images." All the more striking then, the need Miller evidently felt to have the characters stand forth and give their various interpretations of Willy's life after the drama proper has closed with Willy's death. The choruslike effect of the

"Requiem" is obviously related to Miller's conscious effort to write a tragedy of "the common man," a drama which places man in his full social context, which in his essay "On Social Plays" is so clearly associated in Miller's mind with Greek drama. From another point of view the "Requiem" may also be seen as the embryo of the narrator figure who becomes so conspicuous in *A View from the Bridge* and *After the Fall:* after the play is over the characters stand forth and tell the audience what the play is about.

Miller's reluctance to let a play speak for itself became even more evident in his two attempts to add extra material to the original text of *The Crucible* after its first production in 1953. The first of these additions, a second scene in act 2, helps to explain Abigail's behavior in act 3, but, as Laurence Olivier told the playwright, it is not necessary. Although Abigail's psychotic character is brought out entirely in action and dialogue, in an encounter with John Proctor on the eve of the trial, and there is no suggestion of extra-dramatic exposition, the added scene is nevertheless evidence of Miller's sense of not having succeeded in making himself understood in the original version of the play.

More striking is the evidence provided by the series of nondramatic interpolated passages in the first act, where the playwright takes on the roles of historian, novelist and literary critic, often all at once, speaking himself *ex cathedra* rather than through his characters *ex scena*. There is an obvious difference in intent as well as effect in writing an introductory essay to one's play and writing a series of comments that are incorporated in the text itself. The material used need not be different. For example, some of the comments on Danforth in the introduction to the *Collected Plays* are quite similar to those on Parris or Hale incorporated in the play. In the one instance, however, he is looking at his play from the outside, as one of its many critics, in the other he has added new material to the play and has thus changed the text.

In effect the play has a narrator, not realized as a character but present as a voice commenting on the characters and the action and making clear some of the moral implications for the reader/audience. The director of the 1958 Off Broadway revival of *The Crucible* drew the consequences of the revised text and introduced "a narrator, called The Reader, to set the scenes and give the historical background of the play." Besides his function as one of the minor characters, this is what Alfieri does in *A View from the Bridge*. The introduction of a "narrator" element in *The Crucible* is closely related to Miller's attempts to have a separate voice present the author's view of the "generalized significance" of the "action" in the later play.

The interpolated expository passages of *The Crucible* serve two different purposes. Frequently the comments on a character merely repeat points made in that part of the drama which may be acted on the stage. Indeed, the opening words of the following paragraph on John Proctor are sugges-tive of the Victorian novelist guiding his readers through his story, making sure that no point, however obvious, may be missed:

> But as we shall see, the steady manner he displays does not spring from an untroubled soul. He is a sinner, a sinner not only against the moral fashion of the time, but against his own vision of decent conduct. These people had no ritual for the washing away of sins. It is another trait we inherited from them, and it has helped to discipline us as well as to breed hypocrisy among us. Proctor, respected and even feared in Salem, has come to regard himself as a kind of fraud. But no hint of this has yet appeared on the surface, and as he enters from the crowded parlor below it is a man in his prime we see, with a quiet confidence and an unexpressed, hidden force. Mary Warren, his servant, can barely speak for embarrassment and fear.

Proctor's sense of guilt is central to any understanding of him as a dramatic character, but certainly this is made sufficiently clear by, for instance, the several explicit remarks made by Elizabeth as well as by his behavior on the stage.

While such passages are further instances of Miller's apparent distrust of his medium as a means of communication, other passages speak of an impatience with the limitations of the dramatic form. Miller had researched this play thoroughly, and it is as if on second thought he has regretted that he had not been able to bring as much of his research and his historical insights into the play as he would have liked. But when he in the interpolated passages takes on the roles of historian and biographer he tends to confuse the sharp line that must be drawn between the characters in a play called *The Crucible* and a group of late seventeenth century individuals bearing the same names as these characters. Thus, in the first of the two paragraphs that serve to introduce Proctor as he enters on the stage, Miller tells us:

> Proctor was a farmer in his middle thirties. He need not have been a partisan of any faction in the town, but there is evidence to suggest that he had a sharp and biting way with hypocrites. He was the kind of man—powerful of body, even-tempered, and not easily led—who cannot refuse support to partisans with-

out drawing their deepest resentment. In Proctor's presence a
fool felt his foolishness instantly—and a Proctor is always
marked for calumny therefore.

The change in tense in the paragraph that follows (quoted above) suggests
that Miller had a different Proctor in mind in each paragraph: the historical
Proctor and the character in the play. This confusion runs through the
various character sketches or brief essays on for instance Parris, Putnam,
Rebecca and Francis Nurse. It should further be noted that these interpolated
expository passages are often concerned with motivation, and that psychological, religious and socioeconomic explanations of the trials are all given.
While the information is interesting in itself and throws light on the Salem
trials, it cannot add to our understanding of the drama as acted on the stage.
Whatever needs to be known about these characters and their motives by
the audience must be expressed in action and dialogue. That is, if we do
not accept the dichotomy of "action" and "significance," with the latter
element presented by a representative of the author, a "Reader" or a
narrator.

The assumption of such a dichotomy, according to Miller, lies at the
heart of the structure of his next play, *A View from the Bridge*. Here, and
in *A Memory of Two Mondays,* the one-act play originally presented on the
same play bill, Miller thinks of himself as having followed "the impulse to
present rather than to represent an interpretation of reality. Incident and
character are set forth with the barest naivete, and action is stopped abruptly
while commentary takes its place." On the face of it, however, it is difficult
to see why such commentary should be found necessary, unless the playwright had given up trying to make himself understood through "action"
alone or, rather, to let his "action" carry the full weight of the "significance"
he saw in it.

In his introduction Miller claims at the outset that his "approach to
playwriting and the drama itself is organic," and he insists that "the play
must be dramatic rather than narrative in concept and execution." When
towards the end of the introduction he explains that "the organic impulse
behind" his early plays was "split apart" in *A View from the Bridge,* it is as
if he admits the failure of this approach. The organic structure of the early
*All My Sons,* however, has already been questioned by Miller in his critique
of its two centers of interest. As in this earlier play, the emotional center
of *A View from the Bridge* is embedded in the action. But in the latter play
Miller explains that he deliberately tried not to have the dialogue of the
characters involved in the action carry any burden that goes beyond this

action. The aspect of the play that dialogue attempted to express in *All My Sons* is now delegated to the narrator. The more explicit splitting apart of "the organic impulse" has been observed in *Death of a Salesman* with its concluding "Requiem." Moreover, Miller has also been seen to depart from the second of his two basic principles of playwriting in introducing narrative and expository passages into *The Crucible*. With *A View from the Bridge* he wrote a play that approaches illustrated narrative.

Alfieri, the lawyer-narrator, opens the play by telling a little about himself and his neighborhood and suggesting some of the themes of the play to follow. When Eddie appears on the stage, the verbal tense Alfieri makes use of is striking in its implications: "This one's name *was* Eddie Carbone" (my italics). Later in the play Alfieri consistently refers to Eddie in the past tense. The story is obviously Alfieri's story. What we see on the stage is Alfieri's memory of Eddie as he ponders on its significance: "This is the end of the story. Good night," he concludes the original one-act version of the play. The past tense is the mode of narrative; drama is enacted in the present.

The title *A Memory of Two Mondays* is in itself interesting in this connection as it suggests an implied narrator, someone whose memory is projected on the stage as is Alfieri's. This technique is developed to its furthest extreme in *After the Fall*, where "*the action takes place in the mind, thought, and memory of Quentin*." The play has become illustrated narrative, and is essentially a two-act monologue which the narrator and main character Quentin, directs at the audience. Significantly, since the flow of narration is essential to the play and the many dramatizations of situations in the narrative are incidental, Quentin's audience is in Miller's stage directions defined as a "*Listener, who, if he could be seen, would be sitting just beyond the edge of the stage itself.*"

The images presented on the stage are illustrations of Quentin's consciously controlled discourse or of the working of his subconsciousness as he struggles for self-understanding and self-acceptance. In either case, the device of giving characters within "*the mind, thought, and memory of Quentin*" a semi-independent status on the stage and allowing them to speak for themselves makes possible an objective view of the self-image projected by Quentin in his discourse. Essentially, however, Miller has placed a character on the stage and given him the opportunity of examining his life and motives and explaining himself to a Listener through a monologue that lasts the whole length of a two-act play. From point of view of genre the result is a cross between expressionist drama, stream of consciousness novel and dramatic monologue. The result, however, is good theater: It works on the stage. The critical attacks on *After the Fall* have mainly been concerned with Miller's subject matter and theme, not his experiment with dramatic form.

Rather than add a clarifying "Requiem," as he did with *Death of a Salesman;* rather than interpolate expository passages in the published play to make himself more readily understood, as he did in *The Crucible;* and rather than introduce a narrator, somewhat to the side of the central plot, who could explain the author's "reading of its significance," Miller in *After the Fall* made the narrator's attempt to arrive at the significance of his own life and explain himself directly to the audience the center of the play. Ironically, Miller may never have felt himself so misunderstood by audiences and critics alike as after the first production of *After the Fall* in 1964, the play that may be seen as the culmination of a series of efforts to develop a form that would allow him to present his intentions unmistakably and clearly to his public.

Some years earlier, in his introduction to the *Collected Plays,* Miller had observed that "the intention behind a work of art and its effects upon the public are not always the same." His answers to the question of how to avoid this communication gap could not, finally, have struck him as successful in practice. In his next play, at least, *Incident at Vichy,* written immediately after the critical disaster of *After the Fall,* he returned to the form of the straightforward, realistic play. By concentrating on one of the two poorly integrated themes of *After the Fall,* that represented by the concentration camp tower, the later play, moreover, avoids the conflict between two different kinds of "morality" or "motivation" many critics have found in his plays up to and including *After the Fall. Incident at Vichy* may be too much the drama of ideas (and not very new or original ones at that) to be successful in the theater, and Von Berg's development may not be quite convincing on the stage; but at least there is no need for any "Requiem," explanatory footnotes or narrator to express the play's dominantly public theme.

Four years later Miller returned to the material of *All My Sons, Death of a Salesman* and *After the Fall* in another family drama, *The Price.* The play is also a return to the realistic style and retrospective technique of *All My Sons.* But of course Miller had traveled a long distance since 1947. There is a greater economy of characters and incidents, a more subtle and dramatically integrated use of symbols, no more need for manipulative, mechanistic devices like surprise arrivals or unsuspected letters. Two hours in an attic with old furniture and four people—and the experience in the theater is of something organic, something that comes alive and evolves before us on the stage. The playwright appears relaxed, confident that the "action" expresses its "generalized significance": the characters speak for themselves and the play speaks for Arthur Miller.

The critics who found, I think rightly so, a confusion of private-psychological and public-political themes in Miller's plays were addressing themselves to the very problem Miller has repeatedly pointed to as the central one for the dramatist in our day: how to create a form that can bridge "the deep split between the private life of man and his social life." Miller's belief, expressed in several essays in the mid-fifties, that it is the unrealistic modes of drama that are capable of expressing man's social relationships, as opposed to the realistic drama which is best suited to present the private life, is seen most clearly at work in A View from the Bridge from 1955. The "bridge," however, is rather crudely built: to the side of the realistic action stands the narrator, who in the first version of the play spoke in verse—poetry, according to Miller, being the style most closely related to public themes. In the light of such theories the author's misfired intentions with After the Fall, his most "unrealistic" play, may be more easily understood; and the irony of its reception as his most embarrassingly private play more readily appreciated. There is further irony in the successful synthesis of the public and the private spheres in The Price. For according to Miller's theory, the realism of this or any other play "could not, with ease and beauty, bridge the widening gap between the private life and the social life." But in his essay on "The Family in Modern Drama," Miller had also wondered: "Why does Realism always seem to be drawing us all back to its arms? We have not yet created in this country a succinct form to take its place." This was written at a time when Miller was trying to break away from realism. This movement, however, had its temporary conclusion in After the Fall, the play that more than any other must have led Miller to despair of communicating his intentions to his audience.

The ironies of Arthur Miller's career as a dramatist were further compounded with the production of The Creation of the World and Other Business in 1973. In spite of the success, with audiences as well as with critics, of The Price, following the disastrous reception of his experiments in After the Fall, Miller seems unable to rest comfortably in the strong and protective arms of Realism. His latest play is his first attempt to express himself through comedy and pure fantasy, and in this his most radical departure from realism his earlier concern with the problems of integrating man's private and social life has given way to teleological speculation. Behind the fanciful cosmological draperies, however, one may discover the playwright's old story of the two sons and familial conflict. Indeed, the new play serves as a reminder that the Cain and Abel story is an archetypal pattern in *All My Sons, Death of a Salesman, After the Fall* and *The Price*.

In a different guise the old question of the two centers of interest is also raised by Miller's attempt at comedy. While God and Lucifer incessantly come together on the stage to discuss the Creator's design, Miller's alleged theme, the audience, who cannot but grow restless after two acts with God, his Angels and a boring couple named Adam and Eve, are finally given the two sons, the responsible and respected Cain and the irresponsible and loved Abel. The rather simplistic psychological presentation of the conflict between them is the kind of dramatic material Miller has successfully handled before, and both because it is welcome relief from the overall tediousness of the rest of the play and because it has dramatic potential, it will easily lay claim to the attention and the interest of the audience at the expense of the play's concern with the human dilemma. Miller's latest Broadway venture thus is not only thematically related to his first one but shows that the playwright has still not been able to solve the problem of dramatic form he then felt had served to obscure his main theme.

The story of Arthur Miller's struggle with dramatic form had its beginning in his realization of the two centers of interest in *All My Sons*. His subsequent theories of social drama and its relationship to the realistic and unrealistic modes of drama should be regarded primarily as rationalizations of his own attempts to express himself clearly, to bridge the gap not so much between the social and the private as between his conscious intentions and the audience and critical responses. This was fully demonstrated in his attempts deliberately to separate the action of a play from its significance. His distrust of the realistic drama as a usable medium was thus properly a distrust of the theater itself as a medium, as evidenced in his use of intermediary commentary and narrators and in his tendency towards illustrated narrative. Realism nevertheless has proved to have a strong hold on Miller, and it is the mode with which, the evidence of his plays suggests, he is most at home. *The Creation of the World and Other Business* marks a break with the tone and style of all his previous plays, but it is impossible at this point to guess whether it will turn out to be a new departure in his career or a dead end. Although Miller, like the devil in Ibsen's *Peer Gynt,* has not always been able to reckon with his audience, he has demonstrated that he has been extemely sensitive to their responses. He may therefore accept the common verdict of critics and audiences and return to the kind of work that has placed him in the front rank of contemporary dramatists.

# Two Early Plays

*Dennis Welland*

As an undergraduate at the University of Michigan Miller achieved, with at least two plays, a success that did not attend his first Broadway piece, *The Man Who Had All the Luck* (1944). It won a Theatre Guild prize, and the shortness of its run attracted from the *Burns Mantle Yearbook* the comment that this "unusually interesting and well-played comedy was mistakenly withdrawn, it seemed to this writer, after only 4 performances. It was at least worth a three-week chance to find itself and its public." Although Miller chose not to include it in *Collected Plays,* its anticipations of the later works merit discussion.

In the printed version (which is not identical with the version staged) David Frieber, a garage mechanic in a small midwestern country town, prospers in business and in private life by a series of chances, despite a conviction that things must sometime go wrong. Eventually, to satisfy himself that skill matters more than luck and the generosity of his friends that have so far shaped his life, he mortgages everything to start a mink-farm. Adverse weather conditions and a delivery of diseased fish threaten the success of the minks' whelping, on which everything is staked, but disaster might still have been averted were it not that Hester, his wife, sensing his superstition, forces him to let them die: "It's not that they must die. It's that you've got to kill them . . . I want you to know once and for all that it was you who did it." Like the characters in Miller's later plays, though more artificially, David is thus forced into an acceptance of moral responsibility.

From *Miller: A Study of His Plays.* © 1979 by Dennis Welland. Eyre Methuen, 1979.

The play's weaknesses are evident in the first act. The dramatisation of luck is always likely to strain coincidence but here the long arm quickly acquires proportions altogether too simian. Opposition to the orphan David's marriage is eliminated in the opening scene when Hester's father is killed pushing the car on the repair of which David's career is to be based. His technical skill is inadequate to detect and repair the fault in the time given, but it is done for him while he sleeps. We may accept the nocturnal ministrations of fairy-folk in a tale by Grimm, but it is another thing to believe that a newly-arrived garage-proprietor would choose the middle of the night for his first call on a rival and would then be so accommodating as to save the situation for him.

Moreover, the stage is cluttered with a superfluity of minor characters who seem to have moved in from Winesburg, Ohio, and lost something in the process. The crippled storekeeper and David's fuddled aunt serve no real dramatic purpose. The car-owner need not make an appearance at all, and it is prodigal as well as unnecessary to bring Hester's father on the stage for two minutes in order to run him over in the wings as soon as he leaves. It is theatrical tact that is lacking here, and self-confidence. Miller tries to create the sense of a community, a real town, by crowding the stage with people in a spirit of mistaken naturalism. There is no real reason why the opening scene should be a store, but the stage directions are meticulous in their cataloguing of the hardware on display and of the furnishings. In the second scene the car is actually on stage, its engine is started and the repairs are begun in full view of the audience.

At the play's climax, when Hester urges David to let the mink die, sentimental sententiousness takes over. "Davey, you're a good man, good with your hands" equates virtue with dexterity far more portentously than does Linda Loman's praise for the do-it-yourself skill of her salesman husband, who was also "good with his hands." David talks like a character from *The Grapes of Wrath:*

> I stood in the world with money in my hands and everything was "mine!" It was not *mine,* nothing is mine but what I'm good enough to make. Money is a bitch, Hester, it's a whore bitch that'll bear for any man and what it bears can never really be yours. Only these animals are mine. In the whole world they're the only things that would have died if I weren't there to make them live!

The emotionalised stage direction is similarly Steinbeckian: "He turns slowly away toward the open door as though feeling the dying of his mink. She steps away from him as though from a child first learning to stand."

Well-meant indignation and intensity of moral earnestness provide the motivation even in minor aspects. Thus the storekeeper is a war-veteran who has lost his legs and who has been soured both by his disablement and by the irony that it was sustained, not on the battlefield, but after the Armistice when a boiler exploded in a Paris brothel; he has no real relevance to the story and seems to belong with *A Farewell to Arms* rather than to the nineteen-forties. His reiterated opinion that "a man is a jelly-fish washed up on the beach" is repudiated by the play's moral; it is never adequately explored or developed.

## II

Miller remarks that "far from being a waste and failure this play was a preparation and possibly a necessary one, for those that followed." This he connects, somewhat cryptically, with his sudden recognition that "two of the characters . . . were logically brothers and had the same father." When the play was staged the hero's surname was accordingly changed to Beeves. A subplot had already been concerned with Patterson Beeves and his son Amos. Bringing David into the family deprives him of the orphan status that had heightened the fairy-tale quality of the earlier version, but it establishes a dramatic pattern central to much of Miller's work.

Patterson Beeves has devoted his life and energy to the dream of turning Amos into a champion baseball player, only to see him rejected by a talent scout in one of the play's most moving scenes. To Patterson's uncomprehending explanation of the intensive winter indoor training he has devised for the boy, the scout replies: "Yeah, that's just where you made your mistake, Mr. Beeves"; and when Patterson tells him Amos "doesn't know how to do anything else," his reply is the same: "I guess that was another mistake." By making David Amos's brother, Miller gives Patterson one son whom he destroys through a misplaced desire for his success, and another who survives the parental devotion, though he is not unscathed by it. It is the story of the Kellers in *All My Sons* and the Lomans in *Death of a Salesman*. The parallel to the latter is accentuated by the use of the folklore dream of success through prowess on the games-field and by the identical terms of abuse ("fake" and "liar") that both Amos Patterson and Biff Loman apply to their fathers, although Willy's betrayal of Biff is far more complex and more far-reaching morally than Patterson's of Amos.

Whether, in the stage version, David's brother relationship to Amos was emphasised by any other changes, I do not know, but Miller seems to have perceived the theme's full implications only gradually in the first three plays in which it occurs. Of the "destroyed" sons, Amos is passive, dumb and dramatically uninteresting. Larry Keller is dead before the play opens, but his recognition of his father's guilt, conveyed in his letter to his fiancée, is more articulate and more morally perceptive than Amos's. Biff is the most "aware" of the three, the most fully portrayed, and the one whose betrayal disturbs us most.

To the other brother Miller's attitude changes more sharply. David is the play's central figure and the man who had all the luck. Chris Keller is prompted by a stronger moral indignation and is faced with bigger problems: he has learnt in the war that he can fail, but he has also learnt to live with that knowledge and to build on it. He still has a lot of the luck, and he retains something of David's superstitious guilt, though its motivation is made more acceptable by his description to his fiancée, Ann, of the death of his company of soldiers. His idealistic social conscience makes him the object of an envy and a resentment more true-to-life than the benevolence David's luck inspired in his friends. Ann's brother embodies it particularly, but a neighbour has already put it more caustically ("I resent living next door to the Holy Family"), and even Ann warns Chris of his tendency to idealise his friends. In the earlier play David's effect on people is described by his benefactor J. B. Feller: "Everytime I set eyes on him something happens to me. I suddenly feel that everything is possible again." In *All My Sons* this effect becomes more ambivalent.

> SUE (*with growing feeling*): Chris makes people want to be
> better than it's possible to be. He does that to people.
> . . . My husband has a family, dear. Everytime he has a
> session with Chris he feels as though he's compromising
> by not giving up everything for research. As though
> Chris or anybody else isn't compromising.

J. B. Feller and Jim Bayliss, Sue's husband, stand in the same relationship to the younger heroes of the two plays and represent the same values of good-neighbourliness. The difference between them is not merely that an external critic of Jim is provided for us in Sue: in *All My Sons* the claims of family responsibility have become much more complex, and idealism is judged not per se but in terms of the conflicts it provokes.

Chris is the most attractive, the most decent, of the three versions of that character. David is wooden by comparison and less human but, like him, Chris learns a responsible independence. After his confession of guilt it is again the woman who tells him, almost in the words Hester had used: "Because you mustn't feel that way any more. Because you have a right to whatever you have. Everything, Chris, understand that? To me, too . . . And the money, there's nothing wrong in your money." In saying that, Ann knows something of his father's guilt but is realistic enough to recognise that Chris bears no part of it. The change that the Chris-character undergoes, however, before his reincarnation in the next play is striking.

"Happy" Loman has lost all the conscientious scruples of David and Chris to become as demoralised as his brother but in a more cynical way. Happy accepts his father's standards without fighting them, and has the adaptability necessary to make them work for himself. He no longer needs any of the luck: he is the smooth operator who gets what he wants by having the personality to take it. It emerges in his conversation with Biff:

> That girl Charlotte I was with tonight is engaged to be married in five weeks. . . . The guy's in line for the vice-presidency of the store. I don't know what gets into me, maybe I just have an overdeveloped sense of competition or something, but I went and ruined her, and furthermore I can't get rid of her. And he's the third executive I've done that to. Isn't that a crummy characteristic? And to top it all, I go to their weddings!

Of David another character has said that he "is not comfortable unless everybody he knows is as happy as himself. He suffers sometimes from an over-developed sense of responsibility." The change, in what is basically the same character, from "an over-developed sense of responsibility" to "an overdeveloped sense of competition or something" is a convenient index to the shift from inner-direction to other-direction that David Riesman and his collaborators were charting sociologically at about the time that Miller was writing *Death of a Salesman*. It also reflects Miller's maturing disillusion in this David/Chris/Happy character, and even more, his growing awareness of the importance of the father-character.

After *Death of a Salesman* the focus shifts back to the brothers. Quentin and Dan, in *After the Fall,* are contrasted in their attitudes to the father ruined in the Depression. On this identical contrast *The Price* is based, and here the theme receives its fullest treatment: for the first time the father is not seen on stage at all but remains a strongly felt presence throughout. Even in *The Creation of the World and Other Business* the Cain and Abel element explores a similar fraternal antagonism. All these will be discussed in their turn, but *The Man Who Had All the Luck* has other links with *All My Sons.*

### III

Both originated in real-life anecdotes that Miller had heard, both have a midwestern setting and atmosphere, both are cast in the same dramatic mould. The fussily realistic detail of the set recurs in *All My Sons* but this time it is concentrated into one location throughout and an element of symbolism is introduced by the use of the tree. The cast list is smaller than its predecessor by only one, and although the characters are, on the whole, more skilfully utilised, more fully developed, and more dramatically relevant, it is arguable that the sense of a neighbourhood community could have been more economically evoked. The small boy Bert is readily dispensable, and the Lubeys contribute little to the essential action.

Nevertheless, the advance on *The Man Who Had All the Luck* is evident both in theme and technique. An aircraft-engine manufacturer with no conscience who supplies faulty cylinder heads in wartime is likely to command more attention and to raise wider issues than a mink-farming mechanic with a conscience at once too sensitive and too narrow. However, it is primarily at the domestic level that the problem is explored; the real value of the war framework lies in its topicality, in the audience-indignation that is universally generated against Joe Keller, and in the social tension and guilt set up in his sons. But there is never any question of these emotions prompting Chris to any form of political action or public protest—a point too obvious to need making, except that references to the play too often suggest that it is politically directed.

Miller's achievement here, to put it at its lowest, lies in the verisimilitude with which he creates not only a convincing homely family, but also the sense of the flow of communal life in a suburban neighbourhood. The Kellers are part of a town in a way that the Beeves never were. Indeed, the atmosphere of American neighbourliness is allowed to become so predominant that we are not kept sufficiently aware of the latent hostility to Joe that is mentioned from time to time.

Joe himself is too pleasant for the part he has to play. His betrayal of his partner seems out of key with his simple geniality and warmth of nature. As with most of Miller's characters, there is no vice in him, only littleness and his own form of myopia. He is genuinely unable to visualise the public consequences of what was for him a private act. To have stopped production when the flaw was discovered would have endangered the future of the business that meant security for his family: it was as simple as that. Keller is no villainous capitalist egged on by competitive mania in a cutthroat world of business, nor is he the cynical profiteer deliberately reducing the margin of safety in order to increase the margin of profit. Miller sees him as the simple man who has got on by energy and will power but who is hardly clever enough to know how he has done it. To this extent he is another man who has had "all the luck" and there is more than a grain of truth in his wife's comment to their son: "We're dumb, Chris. Dad and I are stupid people. We don't know anything. You've got to protect us." He is the ordinary man, surprised that "every week a new book comes out," occasionally uncertain of his pronunciation, aggressively proud of his night-school education, yet moved to embarrassed facetiousness by his sons's knowledge of French, and perplexed by a world where "you stand on the street today and spit, you're gonna hit a college man." Yet even these traits are only sporadically evident: it is the man's *bonhomie*, sense of fun, and good nature that predominate. If we come to accept the idea of this man deliberately allowing his partner to take the blame for shipping the faulty engines and thinking to patch up his conscience as easily as the flaws were patched to delay detection—and we do accept it in the theatre— it is primarily because of the dramatic effectiveness with which the climax and denouement are brought about. Only later do we realise that it is in character, that it is the reverse of the coin of which the obverse has seemed so attractive, and that the coin is of smaller denomination than we thought, but none the less still a recognisable part of the currency.

The improvement in dramatic effectiveness may be immediately illustrated from the act-endings. In *The Man Who Had All the Luck* the direction *slow curtain* repeated at the end of most of its five scenes recalls too readily Miller the student-dramatist who had had to ask a friend how long an act ought to be. There is not the climactic use of the curtain that is achieved naturally in *All My Sons* even in the first, relatively slow-moving act. The second act is brought to an explosive but perfectly timed conclusion, and the superbly developed tension of the play's ending is blurred only by the bringing of Chris back on to the stage for his mother's final and uncharacteristically wise comment. The impulse to prolong the action of *Death of a Salesman* beyond the death of its protagonist is more defensible than this, if only because the central issue of *All My Sons* is simpler and the suicide of Joe Keller dramatically more self-justifying, for the events leading up to it have been presented with a directness and an increasing tempo that make any alternative impossible. By contrast to Miller's skilful observance of the old unities in *All My Sons* the episodic structure of *The Man Who Had All the Luck,* with its dramatic confusion, loss of pace, and irrelevancies of character and action, seems almost amateurish.

The objection is sometimes made that *All My Sons* is so well-constructed as to be unconvincing, and the delayed revelation of Ann's third-act production of the letter from Larry is instanced as meretricious playmanship. On the other hand, her reluctance to produce it earlier is credibly enough explained by her, and it would not be easy to devise a more economical—or a more telling—method of bringing home the two things essential to the action at that point: the demolition of the mother's dream that her son is still alive and the demonstration to Joe, in terms that he cannot escape, of the consequences of his own conduct. Whether Ann, with that knowledge, would have been quite so sympathetic to Joe earlier in the play is another question, but one that Joe's irresistible geniality and Ann's nostalgia for the past go part of the way to answering, especially as she has earlier accepted the court's verdict that the blame was her own father's rather than Joe's.

The confident certainty of dramatic movement here seems deliberately and successfully counterpoised against the loss of certainty that is the play's main theme. The keynote of the play is its questioning. Dialogue in the theatre is regularly carried on in terms of questions and answers, but in *All My Sons* the questions are in effect dialogue-stoppers. The dramatic power resides in the sort of questions asked and in the inability of the characters to answer them. Particularly prominent in the last act and in the exchanges between Joe and his son, this is observable throughout, and is responsible for the powerful climax to the second act in Chris's agonised reiteration of such questions as "Where do you live, where have you come from? . . . What must I do, Jesus God, what must I do?" Nothing brings out Joe Keller's bewildered isolation better than this exchange with his wife:

> KELLER: Maybe I ought to talk to [Ann]?
> MOTHER: Don't ask me, Joe.
> KELLER (*almost an outburst*): Then who do I ask? But I don't
> think she'll do anything about it.
> MOTHER: You're askin' me again.
> KELLER: I'm askin' you. What am I, a stranger? I thought I had
> a family here. What happened to my family?
> MOTHER: You've got a family. I'm simply telling you that I
> have no strength to think any more. . . .
> KELLER: Then what do I do? Tell me, talk to me, what do I
> do?

A few minutes later, among questions to his son, he interjects the same plea: "Talk to me."

This is the bewilderment of a naturally garrulous man who has suddenly realised the impossibility of communication on the matters of deepest consequence, and it is a dilemma which the often-criticised banality of Miller's dramatic idiom is particularly well suited to suggest. Against these baffled questions and the clichés of his quotidian conversation Joe's final statement in the play stands out with an integrity and a force far in excess of its verbal content. His decision is made and his question answered by the letter of his dead son:

> MOTHER: You're so foolish. Larry was your son too, wasn't he? You know he'd never tell you to do this.
>
> KELLER (*looking at letter in his hand*): Then what is this if it isn't telling me? Sure, he was my son. But I think to him they were all my sons. And I guess they were, I guess they were.

That is almost the only statement in this play of questioning that should be taken at its face value, and its quiet dignity makes Chris's summing-up ("there's a universe of people outside and you're responsible to it") superfluous and gratuitously didactic. The other and more sensational statements must be seen in their immediate context. "This is the land of the great big dogs, you don't love a man here, you eat him! That's the principle"—it is not Miller who says this, but Chris, and Chris the baffled idealist *in extremis*. Its hysterical note distinguishes it from the more responsible tone of genuine recognition in Joe's speech. The play is a social drama, not as an attack on the capitalist business ethic, but as a study of the bewildered common man groping in a world where moral values have become a shifting quicksand, where you ask for guidance from others no surer than yourself, and when the simplest lesson—moral responsibility to others—is the hardest to learn.

# All My Sons

## Leonard Moss

*All My Sons*, Miller's first success on Broadway, represents a considerable advance in the author's ability to manipulate language. To a casual observer the dialogue may appear to be simply a phonographic imitation of a contemporary American idiom, replete with clichés and slang. In the opening scene, comfortable gossip circulated by the Kellers and their friends connotes the sense of security conventionally associated with everyday family and neighborhood life. The talk—ingenuous, friendly, relaxed—duplicates the good-natured banter one might expect to hear in any midwestern suburban backyard on a pleasant Sunday morning.

This deliberate banality, however, encompasses more than mere linguistic verisimilitude: the common man's slangy syntax has been used for theatrical purposes. "The play begins in an atmosphere of undisturbed normality," Miller wrote. "Its first act was later called slow, but it was designed to be slow. It was made so that even boredom might threaten, so that when the first intimation of the crime is dropped a genuine horror might begin to move into the heart of the audience, a horror born of the contrast between the placidity of the civilization on view and the threat to it that a rage of conscience could create" (introduction to the *Collected Plays*). Intruding upon the tensionless domestic world, with its chatter about want ads, parsley, and Don Ameche, a terrible challenge to tranquillity becomes increasingly insistent, finally bursting apart the innocent verbal façade. The peaceful mood deceptively evoked by trite speech prepares the stage for desperate war.

From *Arthur Miller*. © 1980 by G. K. Hall & Co. Twayne Publishers, 1980.

A series of allusions that gradually reveal a hidden sin brings about the transition from tranquillity to fear—an Ibsenesque technique that Miller was to employ in later plays. The Kellers' elder son, Larry, was reported missing in action after a wartime flight; when a neighbor refers to Larry's memorial tree, which was "toppled" by a storm the night before, he sounds the first jarring note. As yet such references do not significantly affect the prevailing conversational tenor, pitched as it is to humorous trivia. Even Joe Keller's teasing a youngster about "jail" contributes to conviviality. But Joe and Chris, his other son, begin to worry about the impact that the tree's destruction will have on Mother, who still hopes for Larry's return. By the time she enters, then, the initial calm has already been somewhat disrupted. Her outburst of grief for the missing flier further disturbs that calm. "Because if he's not coming back," Kate cries, "then I'll kill myself! Laugh. . . . [She points to tree.] Laugh, but there are meanings in such things" (italics are omitted in quoting stage directions here and elsewhere).

Now another complication emerges: Kate refuses to allow Chris to marry his brother's fiancée because that would acknowledge Larry's death. The problem seems to involve mother and son, primarily, with Joe Keller standing by as a concerned spectator: "Well, that's only your business, Chris," he comments. Yet the facts rapidly coming to light in the dozen or more oblique and direct allusions to an old scandal begin to place him in a more central position; they introduce a contradiction between his apparent neutrality and his actual involvement. His former partner in the machine shop, the spectator soon learns, has been serving a prison term for shipping defective cylinder heads that caused the deaths of twenty-one American pilots. "The story was," Keller recalls, "I pulled a fast one getting myself exonerated." And a friend comments, "everybody knows Joe pulled a fast one to get out of jail. . . . There's not a person on the block who doesn't know the truth."

A more dynamic style mirrors the rising apprehension felt by Keller and his wife as their secret rises from the past. Their questions, idly curious before, now become urgently incisive, demanding immediate solution: "Now what's going to happen to Mother? Do you know?" "Why, Joe? What has Steve suddenly got to tell him that he takes an airplane to see him?" "She don't hold nothin' against me, does she? I mean if she was sent here to find out something?" (This last question is answered with another query: "Why? What is there to find out?") The need to "know"—the verb occurs almost two hundred times—assumes first importance. Within a family supposedly united by strong affection there is surprising uncertainty and, therefore, constant inquiry in respect to each other's motives: "I don't understand you, do I?" Keller asks Chris, a comment later echoed by Mother.

The verbal contrast brings out a psychological contrast, as Keller's defensive questions reveal qualities not previously manifested by the industrialist: Harshness starts to displace his simple folksiness, fearfulness displaces the comfortable self-assurance. The grave interrogation alternates with continued small talk. Keller dissembles his growing "nervousness" by performing as a homespun humorist: "I don't know, everybody's gettin' so Goddam educated in this country there'll be nobody to take away the garbage. . . . No kiddin'. It's a tragedy: you stand on the street today and spit, you're gonna hit a college man." But in the second act such pleasantries only bring his terror into sharper relief.

The Kellers attempt to seduce George, the jailed man's son, from his threatening demand for truth with the girl friends, grape juice, and homely clichés that remind him of his carefree existence as a boy in their town. Joe Keller almost succeeds in this verbal enterprise; he woos George with nostalgic reminiscences while discrediting his father with a show of gruff honesty. Then Kate ruins her husband's plan through an incriminating slip of the tongue—a venerable theatrical convention. As excitement builds to a climax, the hectic dialogue mixes the antithetical accents of normalcy and urgency. Keller stubbornly conceals the truth, Kate frantically evades it, and George persistently drives to uncover it ("what happened that day, Joe?"). At the same time, Chris and the neighbors, unaware of the impending crisis, cheerfully pursue avocations ranging from love to astrology.

When Chris discovers that his father had allowed the defective engine parts to be shipped, ordinary speech is unable to carry the intense stress and must be supplemented with exclamation and with violent action. Kate "smashes [Keller] across the face," and Chris in "overwhelming fury . . . pounds down upon his father's shoulder" (author's directions). In a confrontation that climaxes the movement toward revelation at the end of the second act, the son takes up the role of interrogator with a vengeance:

> How could you do that? How? . . . What did you do? Explain it to me or I'll tear you to pieces! . . . God in heaven, what kind of a man are you? . . . Where do you live, where have you come from? . . . What the hell do you think I was thinking of, the Goddam business? Is that as far as your mind can see, the business? What is that, the world—the business? What the hell do you mean, you did it for me? Don't you have a country? Don't you live in the world? What the hell are you? You're not even

an animal, no animal kills his own, what are you? What must I
do to you? I ought to tear the tongue out of your mouth, what
must I do? . . . What must I do, Jesus God, what must I do?

An ethical disparity typical of Miller's "family" plays causes the conflict
between father and son. Joe Keller cares little for public approval, everything
for his son's admiration. To him, "the world had a forty-foot front, it
ended at the building line." "Nothin' is bigger" than the family, in whose
name even homicide can be justified: "My only accomplishment is my son.
. . . There's nothin' he could do that I wouldn't forgive." "Joe Keller's
trouble, in a word," Miller has stated, "is not that he cannot tell right from
wrong but that his cast of mind cannot admit that he, personally, has any
viable connection with his world, his universe, or his society" (introduction
to CP).

If the father is monomaniacal in his loyalty, the son qualifies his familial
devotion. Chris cares for his family—"you're the only one I know who
loves his parents," a friend remarks—but military combat has taught him
a higher principle. The men in his command "killed themselves for each
other. . . . Everything was being destroyed, see, but it seemed to me that
one new thing was made. A kind of—responsibility. Man for man." His
belief recalls Lawrence Newman's final wish for a society founded upon
common welfare rather than upon self-interest and mutual exclusion.

After bringing the conflict to its brilliant culmination, Miller mishan-
dles the resolution. Joe Keller's sudden decision to commit suicide is the
most obvious sign of this mishandling. At first, Keller holds firmly to his
position; his obstinacy impels Chris to curse himself and his father, then
determine to give up his home, career, and fiancée ("now I'm practical,
and I spit on myself"). Instead of sacrificing his own life, however, Chris
brings about his father's death by reading to Joe the letter in which Larry
also had denounced his father and condemned himself. In this way, Chris
damns Keller for Larry's suicide. More than that, the letter apparently
demonstrates the validity of Chris's philosophy on universal brotherhood;
for Keller hints at moral surrender in his cryptic statement before shooting
himself: "Sure, [Larry] was my son. But I think to him they were all my
sons. And I guess they were, I guess they were."

If this vaguely worded last speech is supposed to indicate a sudden
ethical conversion, it hardly suggests the process whereby Keller capitulates
to an alien theory he had savagely resisted until that moment. More likely,
and more appropriately after the gradual increase of tension during the first
two acts, his suicide may be an emotional reaction to the rejection by both
sons (he had warned that, should the bond with his surviving son be severed,

"I'll put a bullet in my head"). But the speech does not express a feeling of deprivation strong enough to overcome Keller's staunch self-defense. The realization that he has driven one son to his death and alienated the other might well be unbearable to a character who has predicated his existence upon pride as a father. Yet the disintegration of such pride seems gratuitous when manifested so casually.

The lameness of the ending is compounded by melodramatic plot devices: One familiar stage convention, an incriminating letter, leads to another, a suicide. Still others occur earlier in the play. There is coincidence: George's crucial interview with his long-imprisoned father takes place at the same time that Chris decides to marry Ann, George's sister. There is a prophetic symbol: The ruined tree portends the death of hope. And there is Kate's fatal slip of the tongue. When such obvious conventions operate in concert with expository methods of some subtlety, as in the first two acts, they remain unobtrusive. When they become the chief narrative means, as in the finale, their awkwardness reaches distressing proportions.

The narrative crudeness and verbal obscurity at the conclusion of *All My Sons* may be symptomatic of a shift in interest from the indignant father to the outraged son. After the last question spoken by Chris in the second act—"what must I do?"—Keller's defense no longer commands central attention. Miller seems to have become captivated by a figure recurrent in his work—a maturing individual (a New-man) who proclaims, in abstract terms, the interdependence of all men. The third act betrays a drift toward the rhetorical style Miller has called upon so freely elsewhere: Sententious declarations delivered by Chris and by three colleagues in disenchantment differ radically in style both from the simple-minded banter prominent in the first act and from the intense exclamation and interrogation prominent in the second.

Keller's attempt to justify his crime remains relatively concrete even when the appeal is made on hypothetical grounds: "Did they ship a gun or a truck outa Detroit before they got their price? Is that clean? It's dollars and cents, nickels and dimes; war and peace, it's nickels and dimes, what's clean?" His questions, now self-answered, continue to expose his apprehension and his toughness; their specificity suits well the narrowness and the urgency of his commitment. On the other hand, Chris, though his diction is plain, argues his case for mutual responsibility with hazy generalities: "Once and for all you can know there's a universe of people outside and you're responsible to it, and unless you know that, you threw away your son because that's why he died." Chris's wider concept is necessarily difficult to explain, but simplification of this kind does not clarify the idea.

No less than three other disillusioned, somewhat pretentious young men express disgust at the selfishness they encounter in the world. In so doing they reinforce the standpoint taken by Chris. Larry posthumously speaks his shame on learning of his father's indictment: "Every day three or four men never come back and he sits back there doing business" (act 3). George has suffered from *his* father's disgrace: "When I was studying in the hospital it seemed sensible, but outside there doesn't seem to be much of a law" (act 2). And Jim gave up the dream of becoming a researcher: "These private little revolutions always die. The compromise is always made. . . . Every man does have a star. The star of one's honesty. And you spend your life groping for it, but once it's out it never lights again" (act 3).

These moralistic speeches place a disproportionate emphasis on the antagonist's position, a change in focus that may account for the inconclusiveness of Keller's presuicide statement, with its token acquiescence in Chris's theory. Besides interrupting the development of the main character, moreover, such judgments dissipate tension. They produce an effect opposite to that achieved early in the play by the judicious alternation of serious and comic moods. After the cleanly decisive second-act clash between father and son, Chris's cynical wisdom comes as a wordy letdown: "We used to shoot a man who acted like a dog, but honor was real there, you were protecting something. But here? This is the land of the great big dogs, you don't love a man here, you eat him! That's the principle; the only one we live by—it just happened to kill a few people this time, that's all. The world's that way, how can I take it out on him? What sense does that make? This is a zoo, a zoo!" (act 3). (Similarly, Sue's long, misleading, and irrelevant criticism of Chris unduly slows the pace after the suspenseful conclusion of the first act.)

The playwright probably directed attention away from the father's loss to the son's in order to show the consequences of a thoroughgoing tribal outlook. "The fortress which *All My Sons* lays siege to," Miller stated, "is the fortress of unrelatedness" (introduction to *CP*). But in taking that course he undercut the source of emotional power he had cultivated during most of the play. *All My Sons,* for two acts an extremely well constructed work, reveals clearly what is evident in almost every play Miller has written—the habit of following a carefully prepared movement to crisis with an anticlimactic denouement. His desire to formulate "social" truths has constricted his talent for capturing inward urgencies in colloquial language.

# Realism and Idealism

## C. W. E. Bigsby

*All My Sons* is ostensibly a play about morality. Joe Keller, a wartime manufacturer of aircraft engines, had been charged with supplying defective equipment which led to the deaths of twenty-one pilots. At the trial, however, he had denied responsibility, allowing his timid partner to take the blame. Having been exonerated, he has successfully reestablished his business and though his neighbours still believe him to be guilty they have apparently accepted him back into their social life. But relief at his acquittal is tempered by grief at the loss of his son, himself a pilot, reported missing, presumed dead.

At the time of the play, some three years later, that son's fiancée, Ann (daughter of Joe Keller's business partner), arrives to become engaged to the dead boy's brother, Chris Keller. This provokes a crisis for his mother, since she has refused to accept the fact of her son's death and has seen Ann's failure to marry as evidence of her similar faith in his survival. The planned marriage, therefore, involves laying the ghost of the dead son. But, more significantly, acceptance of her son's death also forces her to acknowledge a connection between that event and what she knows to be her husband's guilt. The situation is compounded when Ann's brother George arrives to confront Joe with that guilt. And though he fails to wring a confession from Joe the imminent marriage does. For Chris's mother plays her final card in order to prevent the marriage which will signal the end of her hope.

From *A Critical Introduction to Twentieth-Century American Drama 2: Tennessee Williams, Arthur Miller, Edward Albee.* © 1984 by C. W. E. Bigsby. Cambridge University Press, 1984.

She reveals her husband's guilt to her son. But she and her husband are finally defeated by a letter which Ann now reveals, a letter in which the missing son had announced his intention of committing suicide because of his father's actions. Stunned into accepting responsibility for his actions, Joe Keller shoots himself, bequeathing a kind of freedom to his son, who will accept no other inheritance.

On the surface the play is an extension of earlier themes. It is an assertion of the need for the individual to accept full responsibility for his actions, to acknowledge the reality of a world in which the idea of brotherhood is an active principle rather than a simple piety. It is an assault on a materialism which is seen as being at odds with human values, on a capitalist drive for profits which is inimical to the elaboration of an ethic based on the primacy of human life and the necessity to acknowledge a social contract. Indeed Joe Keller defends himself by insisting that his own values are those of the world in which he moves. As he asks, rhetorically, "Who worked for nothing in that war? When they work for nothing, I'll work for nothing. Did they ship a gun or a truck outa Detroit before they got their price? Is that clean? It's dollars and cents, nickels and dimes; war and peace, it's nickels and dimes, what's clean? Half the goddamn country is gotta go if I go." And his son is forced to acknowledge this, lamenting that "this is the land of the great big dogs, you don't love a man here, you eat him! That's the principle; the only one we live by—it just happened to kill a few people this time, that's all. The world's that way, how can I take it out on him?" Yet he still continues to press his demand of the ideal until his father can no longer live with his guilt and his suddenly intensified sense of loneliness. And this is the basis of the play's submerged theme—a concern with guilt as a principal mechanism of human behaviour, and with self-interest as a spectre behind the mask of idealism.

Clearly *All My Sons* rests very squarely on Ibsen's work, and in particular on *The Wild Duck*. This also had taken as its subject two businessmen, one of whom had allowed the weaker partner to go to prison for a fraud which he had himself condoned and probably initiated. He, like Joe Keller, had thrived as a consequence and, despite suspicions, won his way back into public regard. His son's suspicions cast a pall over his success and over his own imminent marriage which he hopes will finally expunge the memory of his first wife who had rightly accused him of betraying her. But Ibsen's emphasis is less on the relationship between father and son than it is on the nature of a supposed idealism itself. The son, Gregers Werle, is seized with what a benign doctor, Relling, calls "acute rectitudinal fever." He wishes to destroy all illusions in the belief that truth has a transcendent value, and that it provides the only basis for human life, but that idealism is seen to be an uneasy compound of guilt and naivety. In denying people their illusions he denies them also their life. And the consequence is the death of a young girl. But the play is by no means simply a defence of what Ibsen called "life-lies" and O'Neill "pipe dreams." Certain illusions are patently destructive, as is Gregers's belief in his own innocence and his consequent assurance about the virtue of truth. Blind to his own self-deception, he becomes a huckster for truth at the expense of human values. In a world whose physical and moral boundaries are shrinking (the natural world has shrunk for the Ekdals to a simulated woodland recreated in their attic), those values become the crucial defence against material and physical constriction.

In Miller's play, too, there is an intricate tracery of self-justification. Most crucially, Chris's idealism conceals a compulsive need to justify his own silence, the suppression of his own doubts. The fact that he has refused to allow his father to add his name to that of the family firm is indicative of his own suspicions. Yet he has continued to draw money from the company. To accuse his father is, ultimately, to affirm his own innocence. So, too, his desire to force his mother to acknowledge his brother's death is less a consequence of his belief in the necessity for truth than a product of his desire to marry that brother's fiancée. Like so many of Miller's characters, his actions are dictated by his desire to "build something," even at the expense of others. Thus, his own repressed self-doubts about his involvement with business lead him to convince his doctor neighbour that he should abandon his practice for research. As a consequence the man leaves his wife for a while only to return with a brooding sense of dissatisfaction.

But Chris is not the only character whose actions are dictated by guilt. Joe Keller himself offers to help his partner and his son, as Ibsen's Werle had done in *The Wild Duck*. His wife struggles to maintain the fiction that her son is alive rather than admit to her husband's guilt and acknowledge her own status as a beneficiary of that crime. And, more crucially, Ann herself finally insists on showing both Joe and his wife their son's letter, partly in order to facilitate her own marriage and partly to purge her own sense of guilt. For she, like her brother, whose own concern with pressing the cause of justice is not remote from his own shame, has not visited or corresponded with her father since his imprisonment. To Joe Keller's appeal to "see it human" they all react in some fundamental way out of a need to justify themselves. The play is thus concerned with an egotism much more basic than that displayed by a materialistic society. This fact is identified but not examined. His characters move in a world of failed dreams; they are betrayed by time and event, desperately bending the world to accommodate their need for meaning and companionship. They see themselves as victims and struggle to find happiness and purpose in adapting themselves to the given. But Miller leaves us with only a series of paradoxes which are dramatised but not analysed. For in suggesting that all actions are rooted in self-concern he comes close to destroying the moral values which elsewhere he wishes to invoke. Morality is at one moment seen as external to individuals, who, deeply flawed, can scarcely elaborate a system of ethics which could only be an expression of that fallibility; at other times it is seen as being defined precisely in terms of the internal needs of those individuals, and hence subject to human imperfection. Morality as absolute; morality as relative.

The immorality of Joe Keller in forwarding defective goods is manifest, but his accusers can invoke no moral system by which to indict him, not because he inhabits a society in which such pragmatism is a norm but because there is no one in the play who can level the accusation without confessing to his or her own self-interest. It was a dilemma to which he would return in *After the Fall,* but in *All My Sons* not only does he not have an answer to the moral dilemma which he has created, he does not even seem fully aware of the nature of the problem which he has posed. For, if idealism and demands for justice must necessarily be flawed, on what grounds can any accusation be legitimately levelled? On the other hand, Chris's belief in human responsibility, reflected in the play's title and Joe Keller's final and dramatically crucial realisation that the pilots whom he indirectly killed were "all my sons," was born less out of this latter confession than out of an event in his own past, the loss of virtually all the members of his company during the war: "I got an idea—watching them go down. Everything was being destroyed, see, but it seemed to me that one new thing was made. A kind of responsibility. Man for man." But there is a suggestion that this too derives from guilt—the guilt of the survivor, for "they didn't die; they killed themselves for each other. I mean that exactly; a little more selfish and they'd've been here today." His survival thus becomes tinged with a suggestion of selfishness which is compounded by his subsequent financial security. "I felt wrong to be alive, to open the bank-book, to drive the new car, to see the new refrigerator." However the connection between idealism and guilt which he proposes is simply assumed; it is not traced to its origin in a model of human nature. In the earlier plays the impulse to transform the self and society had a purity denied here. Of course the war itself offers a potential explanation but the nature of the transformation which he implicitly proposes is not scrutinised. Some thirty years later Miller admitted to the significance of this submerged theme and to his fascination with the guilt of the idealist, but insisted that the sheer pressures of the moment, the immediate context of the war, made it impossible for this to break surface. Indeed he saw a similar logic behind the success, several decades after its first performance, of the Israeli production. The issue of war profiteering was simply too powerful in such an environment to permit more subtle and more disturbing questions to coalesce.

Both *The Wild Duck* and *All My Sons* end with a pistol shot. Gregers Werle remains undeflected from his destructive idealism; the dead girl's father seems likely to lapse back into his self-deceiving torpor. Only the doctor remains clear-sighted, aware of the constant battle between the real and the ideal. In *All My Sons* we are left with an irony which is worrying because Miller remains equivocal in his commitment to it. Thus, a second before his father's suicide, Chris, who has precipitated that suicide, announces that "You can be better! Once and for all you can know there's a universe of people outside and you're responsible to it." In one sense this is clearly the moral of the play, but when the pistol shot rings out it is equally plain that his insistence on the moral has killed his father. When asked by his mother whether he was trying to kill his father with the truth, he had replied, "What was Larry to you? A stone that fell into the water? It's not enough for him to be sorry. Larry didn't kill himself to make you and Dad sorry." But seconds later, with his father dead, he says, "Mother, I didn't mean to." The equivocation is not merely Chris's, it is equally Miller's whose title announces *All My Sons* but whose play proposes an unbridgeable gulf between people and undercuts the very moral necessities he identifies. That contradiction could have become the basis for a more profound play. That it did not was perhaps an indication that the problem remained for him an intractable one until *After the Fall* in 1964, by which time he was clearer as to his view of human fallibility, personal betrayal and a continued commitment to the ideal, and less destabilised by the moral exigencies generated by the war.

*All My Sons* poses a further problem. It implies a critique of society and yet in effect identifies no way in which that society can be transformed. As Miller himself confessed more than thirty years later, "The argument that the Marxists had quite rightly, with that play, was that the son who brings down the wrath of the moral god, remains inside the system which has created this immorality. That's perfectly true. However, I believed then that with a sufficient amount of rigorousness those crimes could be resisted." It was a conviction which remained at the level of rhetoric. It never transformed itself into social action or dramatic effect. But Miller was less concerned with challenging the structure of American society than with revivifying a moribund liberalism, a capitalism purged only of its more evident rapacity.

*All My Sons* is a classically well-made play. With its concealed letters and hidden truths suddenly flourished at moments of dramatic effect, it recalls an earlier theatre. Its success plainly owed something to its topicality. Its melodramatic flavour reflected a public predilection for moral absolutes. Its resentments were those of the community at large who suspected, rightly enough, that profit rather than national interest had motivated many of those who risked capital rather than their lives. And, if there was, at another level, a profound ambiguity about the motives of those who flourished truth as a banner of their innocence, this had rather more to do with the play's literary origins in Ibsen than Miller's conscious concern with dissecting a certain failure at the heart of the liberal impulse. It is true that this would become increasingly important, but now the times seemed to demand some act of reconciliation, while the play's form, the very neatness of its construction, seemed to close the spaces against ambiguity, to deny that very moral incompletion which later became a principal subject of a writer for whom the social, the economic and the political increasingly seemed no more than symptoms of an imperfect human nature drawn equally to the delusive satisfactions of the self and the genuine transcendence of love.

# The Dramatic Strategy of *All My Sons*

*June Schlueter*

*All My Sons* relies on coincidence and contrivance. The play works in production, when an audience is more likely to excuse heavy-handedness and yield to the drama's emotional power. But as text, it cannot cover its seams, and a reader may well be disturbed by Kate's casual remark that her husband hasn't been sick in fifteen years—which leads to the discovery of his lie; by Annie's long-concealed letter from Larry, which clears up the doubt concerning his disappearance; and by Keller's sudden remorse and suicide.

Despite these remnants of nineteenth-century conventions, however, and their seeming incompatibility with the twentieth-century realistic play, Miller crafts his drama deftly, drawing for its structure on the retrospective technique that has come to be identified as "Ibsenesque." In such a structure, the past continually intrudes upon the present, and the exposition often sustains itself through the final act, when the critical piece of information necessary for the play's dramatic ending is revealed. Miller found such a structure particularly hospitable for this story, which insists on the consequences of past action. As Miller notes in the introduction to *Collected Plays,* the question was not whether Keller or Chris could ameliorate the consequences of the crime: "The stakes remaining are purely the conscience of Joe Keller and its awakening to the evil he has done, and the conscience of his son in the face of what he has discovered about his father. . . . The

From *Arthur Miller,* edited by June Schlueter and James K. Flanagan. © 1987 by Crossroad/Ungar/Continuum.

113

structure of the play is designed to bring a man into the direct path of the consequences he has wrought."

Throughout *All My Sons,* Miller works gradually at bringing the audience's level of awareness to that of those in the drama: Keller knows he is responsible for the pilots' deaths; he knows why his wife must continue to believe her son is alive; and he knows that his neighbors know of his guilt. Similarly, Keller's wife, Kate, shares this knowledge. On the other hand, Chris, whose level of awareness coincides with that of the audience, has believed in his father's innocence and tries in earnest to persuade his mother to accept Larry's death. Annie, who returns to the Keller household after several years' absence, has adjusted to the death of her sweetheart, Larry, and is now ready to turn her affections to Chris. She, it turns out, possesses the critical piece of information about Larry's death, which places her above all the other characters in one respect, but, until the play is well under way and her brother George appears, she does not know that her father is serving the prison sentence that is rightfully Keller's. As the play proceeds, providing information to Annie and Chris and, with respect to Larry's death, to Joe and Kate, the audience adjusts its perspectives to accommodate the new evidence, becoming increasingly suspicious of Keller's integrity. With Chris and Annie, it discovers Keller's guilt, and, with Joe and Kate, it learns that Keller's action was responsible for the death of his own son as well.

*All My Sons* takes place in late August, three and one-half years after the loss of the twenty-one pilots and the report that Larry was missing in action. Within twenty-four hours of play time, the Kellers' lives move from tranquillity to calamity, from ignorance or denial of the truth to discovery or admission. The action takes place in the Kellers' backyard, a typically American setting with trees and lawn and a sheltered cove in which Keller relaxes with the Sunday paper. Neighbors on both sides—Jim and Sue Bayliss and Frank and Lydia Lubey—feel free to stop by to share the paper or to chat, lending assurance of the perfectly normal routine of this family's comfortable life.

But act 1 gradually prepares its characters for the catastrophe that will follow, teasing its audience with sour notes that intrude upon this atmosphere of normality. When Frank stops by, he notices what an audience would also have noticed immediately: The slender apple tree downstage left lies toppled, a casualty of the previous night's storm. Keller and son worry about how Kate will respond to the destruction of the tree the family planted in tribute to Larry. As it turns out, Kate already knows about the tree, having witnessed its fate at four A.M., when a vision of Larry flying high above the house in his plane urged her outside. Kate becomes an important figure in the opening act, creating interest through her stolid refusal to accept Larry's death and her repeated insistence that he may yet return. At her request, Frank has been working on Larry's horoscope, which, if it shows that the fatal day in November was a "favorable" day for Larry, will reinforce her hope. Kate's obsession only deepens when Larry's old girlfriend, Annie, returns for a visit at Chris's invitation; she strenuously opposes an alliance between her second son and the woman she still perceives as "Larry's girl."

The effect of such early interest in Kate and in the developing conflict between her and her son Chris over Annie is to delay the interest the play will gradually but forcefully develop in Keller, who will prove to be the central character—one of the first in a line of strong-willed, self-deluded men who typify Miller's vision of the American family. Such a masculine figurehead is both its backbone and its bane. But there are hints in act 1 that Joe will be at the center of the drama. Bert, one of the neighborhood boys, rushes into the Keller yard speaking of law breakers and law enforcers and begging to see the prison in the Keller basement. Keller knows the terms of the game he has encouraged in the neighborhood, but he laughingly sends the boy off without showing him the jail. Speaking delightedly about this game to his wife, Keller explains that the kids took an interest in him when he returned from the penitentiary, but then they began confusing the former inmate with the detective. Kate is quick to correct Keller, suggesting it was not *they* who got confused. The game her husband plays has much to do with his own history, which naturally becomes part of the discussion with the long-absent Annie. Deever, whom Annie and her brother have disowned and whom Keller calls a "little man," is in jail, the consequence of Keller's deliberate confusion of the facts. The criminal became the law enforcer, misrepresented the facts, and assumed the role of the innocent. Upon his return from jail following his exoneration, Keller got out of his car at the corner so he could walk the distance of the block, his head held defiantly high against the neighbors' scorn. But since then, poker games and neighborly rapport have been restored, and the criminal has become the pillar of society.

Similarly, Chris speaks of his days in the army, where he led a corps of men who displayed uncommon friendship and loyalty, defending their colleagues even at the expense of their own lives. Because he escaped the fate of so many of them, Chris feels a vague sense of guilt over his own survival. Though too early in the play to make the connection explicitly, this introspective moment offers a contrast to the guilt-free Keller, who has unconscionably let Deever take the blame. And then Kate responds twice with a disturbing anger, an insistence so impassioned as to be suspicious. She reprimands the child for believing there is a basement jail, then returns to Keller's curious question, the central question of the play, "What have I got to hide?" And when Kate defends her belief in Larry's survival, she reminds her husband, with uncommon intensity, that he above all has got to believe.

By the end of act 1, the audience is sure the play will be Keller's and is anxious about the turn of events. Annie's brother, George, having traveled seven hundred miles from New York to Columbus to tell his father of Annie's impending marriage, telephones. He is coming to the Keller's home, apparently with some new and disturbing knowledge. Alone on stage, Kate and Keller react. Kate fears George's arrival and cautions her husband to be smart. Keller is angry, arrogant, and self-assured. The call redirects attention to the case of the cracked cylinders and to the question of what Keller has to hide.

Miller's second act offers an effective balance of bitterness and sweetness, of anxiety and relief, prolonging its two dramatic questions: How will Annie react to George's belief in his father's innocence—will she still marry into the family that is "covered with blood"—and how will Keller react—will he admit he framed his partner? Was he, in fact, responsible for the shipment of the cylinders? The act takes place later that day, at twilight. Chris is sawing off the broken apple tree and suggesting to his mother that without it there is more light. The atmosphere is one of anticipation: They are waiting for the arrival of George, whom Jim has gone to fetch at the station. Chris, assured in his belief that the family has nothing to hide, seems unconcerned, but Kate is overreacting, pleading with Chris to protect them. She fears the case will be reopened and that Deever's story—that Keller made him do it—will prevail. Near hysteria, she begs Chris to help them—and to send Annie home, for she is of the Deever clan, which hates them. Keller, by contrast, is not worrying, or at least he is expressing his concern more passively—through sleeping.

In the moments before George's arrival, though, even as Keller sleeps, the father-son conflict so familiar to readers of Miller begins to take form. Annie has a chance conversation with neighbor Sue about Chris, which is especially revealing. She dislikes Chris for his idealism and proceeds to impute a fundamental dishonesty to him since he, despite his "holiness," still works in his father's business. Clearly, the neighbors have never believed in Keller's innocence and now resent not only his freedom at the expense of Deever but Chris's acceptance of the tainted firm as the source of his livelihood even as he silently preaches perfection.

Annie, upset, immediately confronts Chris with Sue's opinions, which Chris dismisses as just that. Chris, after all, is attached to his parents, and his love for his father is particularly—and reciprocally—intense. Keller, in fact, has worked all his life for his sons, and, with Larry gone, his hopes rest completely in Chris. Earlier in the play, when Chris appealed to Keller to side with him in his desire to marry Annie, he threatened to leave the business if Keller did not support his cause, and the astonished father capitulated. Keller's need to leave his life's effort as a legacy to his son anticipates a similarly intense—and misdirected—desire in Miller's later central character, Willy Loman. As with the deluded salesman, Keller must have his son be heir or see the commitment of his life invalidated. With Willy, a dream is at stake, but with Keller, Chris's participation in the family business is all that keeps the older man from being a murderer. When, later in the play, Keller confesses his treachery, he justifies it in terms of the prospect of losing his life's work, of robbing himself of the legacy he has promised his sons. He shipped out the risky cylinder heads so he could buy time to prove his business viable and to preserve the business for Chris. Yet Keller still calls the firm J. O. Keller, not J. O. Keller & Son; despite Chris's commitment to the firm, his name has not yet been attached to it. George makes a point of this a bit later, understanding that, though Chris may defend his father as head of the "Holy Family," what is at least an unconscious doubt has prevented him from becoming a partner. Chris can barely assimilate his father's later plea: "I did it for you."

Just before George's arrival, then, a gossipy neighbor has set up the father-son relationship that is central to a play that is, finally, a story of fidelity and belief. Bert believes there is a prison under the Keller house, despite Kate's testimony to the contrary. Yet Kate holds a more dangerous, adult delusion: that her husband is innocent, her son Larry alive. In the first instance, she knows that belief in Keller's innocence necessitates a lie, and she has, for over three years, pretended to others what she has never been able to pretend to herself. But believing in Larry's survival is a bit more manageable, for she has no proof to the contrary. Over the years, though, Kate has connected the events so inextricably that her profession of faith in Larry has become a surrogate expression of faith in her husband. Like Keller, she serves the image of the American family as sacrosanct; neither is willing to admit that their Holy Family is headed by a moral weakling, a man whose culpability is compounded by his refusal to admit his wrong. Neither Keller nor Kate is so self-deluded as to believe their own protestations of innocence, but their belief in the sanctity of the Keller family motivates their perpetuation of the lie. Chris is heir to his parents' principles and morality, yet, being an honest man and an idealist, he can believe only in the purity of his father's behavior. His is the more treacherous kind of self-delusion, for Chris believes religiously in the lie. He never suspected his father's guilt because he could not accommodate that guilt with his vision of self or of family. With his parents, he has joined in the lie—though clearly without any awareness that he is doing so. The neighbors, by contrast, are aware of Keller's guilt, of Kate's cover-up, and of Chris's ignorance by design; they admire Keller's cunning but detest his morality. Yet still, in deference to some abstract concept of neighborliness, they chat with the Kellers and even pretend to trust Joe at cards. Only Annie and George seem to accept the loss of faith attendant upon their father's conviction. They assume the law is right and disown their father as a moral weakling who has committed an unconscionable crime.

The play is a web, then, of homespun fidelities, of faith placed and misplaced, a network of belief that, like the apple tree, snaps under pressure. And the arrival of George begins the weakening of several of the strands, for it prompts Sue to speak contemptuously to Annie of Chris's "phoney idealism," and it reveals the restoration of George's belief in his father.

Deever, of course, has been the victim of the Keller family's deception, and now George has just returned from telling his father that Annie is about to marry into that family. George is himself a lawyer, a man who should see clearly the difference between right and wrong but who has himself been duped for years, too ready to accept Joe's story over his father's. Tellingly, he enters the Keller household wearing his father's hat—and he has come to take Annie home. This time, George believes his father's story. After three and a half years, he now sees his father as Keller's victim and refuses to allow the moral taint of the Keller family to claim his sister. But, even here, Miller does things gradually: Though vehement and bitter when he enters, George falls prey to nostalgia, to Kate's charm, and to the weaknesses he knows his father possesses. Joe's tactic is to welcome George with warmth, arranging a meeting with Lydia, his former girlfriend; to discredit Deever by cataloging other moments of his weakness; and to extend himself generously, offering Deever a position with the firm when in a year or two he gets out of jail. Kate works at George's sense of nostalgia; the two were always friends, and she has remembered to provide him with his favorite grape juice.

The seduction is too much for George, and the bitter reunion turns into a sweet one, with talk of childhood experiences and preparations for the evening meal. Relaxed and appeased, George confesses he never felt at home anywhere but there. He compliments Kate on her youthful appearance and tells Joe he is "amazingly the same." Keller responds by saying he has no time to get sick, and then Kate, endorsing her husband's pride in his good health, speaks the fatal line: "He hasn't been laid up in fifteen years," breaking the spell. Despite Joe's immediate qualification—"Except my flu during the war"—George is alert and challenging, for it was Keller's alleged illness that kept him from the plant on the day the cracked cylinder heads came off the line. Ironically, at the moment when the Kellers are threatened so darkly and so inescapably, at the moment when Kate's worst fears are about to be realized, Miller brings Frank onstage with the announcement that he has completed Larry's horoscope: November 25 was a "favorable" day; Larry must be alive.

But Larry is about to die, for Kate's belief in him need not be sustained beyond the revelation of her husband's guilt, which George's anger now presages. Kate and George both want Annie to leave, but Chris reacts with passion, prohibiting further mention of Larry and directing George to leave. Annie joins Chris in telling her brother to go.

In the quarrel between Kate and Chris that ensues, Kate finally reveals the truth:

> MOTHER: Your brother's alive, darling, because if he's dead,
> your father killed him. Do you understand me now? As
> long as you live, that boy is alive. God does not let a son
> be killed by his father. Now you see, don't you? Now
> you see.

Defeated, Keller pleads that his son never flew a P-40, then justifies his decision: Forty years of his life were at risk the day he ordered the cylinders shipped; he took the chance for Chris's sake. But Chris's sense of moral responsibility, unlike his father's, extends beyond the personal, beyond the family to the larger family of which he felt a part during the war.

Father and son collide over an issue that will resonate through Miller's plays: the conflict between the social and the personal. In this play, as in others that Miller will later write, a man's personal integrity, even his survival, depends on his denial of his social responsibility. Had Keller not wanted so desperately to pass on the family business to his son, he might not have been so profit-oriented as a businessman. He might have halted production of the cylinders and not met the government contract, despite the financial consequence. But, yielding to individual and family pride, he risked processing the faulty parts and lost the bet. Then, faced again with a moral crisis—whether to confess his complicity or look to Deever as a scapegoat—he chose the latter, necessitating a life of deception afterwards.

Once Chris understands what his father has done, once he has identified the heinous consequences of Keller's having placed the personal above the social, the final act moves inexorably toward restitution of the social order through the offender's death. Keller leaves in his wake the broken relationship between Annie and Chris, a dead son, and a family fallen like the apple tree; the sense of a moral and social order prevails.

Keller's guilt established, the dramatic question shifts from "What does Joe Keller have to hide?" to "What will happen now that everyone knows?" Act 2, like act 1, ends with a heavy curtain, Chris pounding his fist on his father's shoulder and weeping, not knowing what to do.

Several hours pass during the interlude between acts, bringing the play's action to 2 A.M. the following day. Act 3 opens with the contemplative Kate rocking on the porch chair, in moonlight. She is waiting for Chris to return. Jim talks with her as she rocks, revealing that the neighbors always knew and assuring her that Chris will come back. While they wait, the elder Kellers try to salvage what is left of their lives, Joe turning meekly to Kate for guidance and she counseling yet another lie: If he told Chris he was willing to go to prison, Chris surely would not ask him to go, but perhaps he would forgive him. Even now, Keller cannot accept responsibility, self-righteously asking what there was that Chris needed to forgive. Acknowledging Kate as the accomplice that she undoubtedly has been, he characteristically shifts the blame once again, faulting her for wanting money. Kate sees that her husband is trying to exonerate himself on familial grounds: "Joe, Joe . . . it don't excuse it that you did it for the family," but Keller insists, "It's got to excuse it!"

The moment is more critical for Keller than the revelation of his guilt in the earlier act. As Miller notes in the introduction to *Collected Plays*,

> Joe Keller's trouble, in a word, is not that he cannot tell right from wrong but that his cast of mind cannot admit that he, personally, has any viable connection with his world, his universe, or his society. He is not a partner in society, but an incorporated member, so to speak, and you cannot sue personally the officers of a corporation.

Keller has always believed in the family as an autonomous entity and the highest principle:

> Nothin's bigger than that. . . . I'm his father and he's my son, and if there's something bigger than that I'll put a bullet in my head!

Within the hour, Keller does put a bullet in his head, in a gesture that both insists on his own belief in family and tentatively acknowledges that his sons, Chris and Larry, may be right in seeing something bigger. Unwilling to relinquish his belief, Keller argues with Chris when he returns, defending himself as a man no worse than others. Ironically, Chris never measured him against other men, never even saw him as a man but only as his father, and until the revelation of act 2, Chris's vision of Keller coincided with his abstract ideal. His philosophy of family affirmed his father's, but now Chris understands what he had known in his army days and had ignored—intentionally or unintentionally—since the court case: that there is something bigger than the family. It is a belief endorsed by brother Larry, through the letter he wrote to Annie on the day of his suicide, which Chris now reads aloud. Larry could not live with the shame of his father's involvement in the deaths of his fellow men. Keller understands that to Larry, "they were all my sons. And I guess they were, I guess they were."

In "The Family in Modern Drama," Miller avers that all great plays deal with a single problem:

> How may a man make of the outside world a home? How and in what ways must he struggle, what must he strive to change and overcome within himself and outside himself if he is to find the safety, the surroundings of love, the ease of soul, the sense of identity and honor which, evidently, all men have connected in their memories with the idea of family?

By the time Keller has the capacity to acknowledge his membership in a larger, social family, whose principles, when in conflict with those of the private family, must prevail, he has already so violated its moral assumptions that even a prison sentence will not absolve him. To Miller, Keller threatens society not because he has sold faulty parts to the military but because that crime has "roots in a certain relationship of the individual to society, and to a certain indoctrination he embodies, which, if dominant, can mean a jungle existence for all of us no matter how high our buildings soar" (introduction to *Collected Plays*).

If there is hope for redemption among the remaining Kellers at play's end, that hope rests in Chris, who ends the act sobbing at Kate's feet as she frees him to live. Chris will leave the Keller household, he will not marry Annie, and he will renew the lesson of his army days that his father—and Willy Loman after him—had such a difficult time learning. For Miller, the struggle between father and son "for recognition and forgiveness," in both *All My Sons* and *Death of a Salesman*, is insufficient: "But when it extends itself out of the family circle and into society, it broaches those questions of social status, social honor and recognition, which expands its vision and lifts it out of the merely particular toward the fate of the generality of men" ("The Family in Modern Drama," *The Theater Essays of Arthur Miller*).

# Bad Faith and *All My Sons*

*Steven R. Centola*

The broad social implications of an individual's bad faith are examined in
*All My Sons,* Arthur Miller's first critically and commercially successful
full-length play. According to Miller, *All My Sons* "is designed to bring a
man into the direct path of the consequences he has wrought . . . [to show]
that consequences of actions are as real as the actions themselves" (introduction, *Collected Plays*). One of the first characters in Miller's canon to
bring about his own destruction by succumbing to a life of bad faith—that
is, a life based on lies and self-deception, Joe Keller futilely tries to deny
his freedom and responsibility for the consequences of his actions. In Miller's
view, Keller makes himself "a threat to society" by choosing to live in bad
faith. Miller explains that Keller endangers society not only because he sells
defective airplane parts to a nation at war, but also because "his cast of
mind cannot admit that he, personally, has any viable connection with his
world, his universe, or his society." Such "unrelatedness" as Keller's is
dangerous, adds Miller, because it can ultimately lead to "a jungle existence
for all of us," an existence that represents not just the end of civilization
but perhaps the end of humanity as well. In this respect, then, *All My Sons*
broaches a subject that will be explored again and again in Miller's later
drama—a subject which transcends the play's obvious social considerations.
As C. W. E. Bigsby points out, in *All My Sons* Miller's "concern with
identity, guilt and the need to reaffirm innocence indicates that for him the
social and psychological could ultimately be traced to their source in the
metaphysical."

---

To dramatize the devastating effect of bad faith in a way that seems credible to his audience, Miller endows his characters with all the contradictions of real people. The Kellers simultaneously seek the love and affection of other people while retreating farther and farther from the outside world back into their own private "fortress of unrelatedness" (introduction to *CP*). Their love and fears, dreams and delusions, lies and self-deception are enacted in an outpouring of human feeling that floods the stage in sweeping surges, propelling the action forward and carrying the audience along in the incessant tide of emotion. Joe and Kate Keller are handled particularly well in this play. Miller's fine ear for speech rhythms allows him to individuate these characters by giving each one distinctive phrasing and intonation. In fact, Miller captures not only the voice but also the gestures, the body movements, the entire physical presence of these people who are tortured by their painful inner struggles. Their dialogue generally helps to convey what is already evident in their outward physical appearance, but at times seems to contradict what is apparent externally because the characters try to conceal their anguish from themselves and each other by pretending that they have no problems. However, this disparity only increases the already heightened tension in the play by amplifying the incongruity between reality and illusion for these characters, thereby revealing the extent to which they have allowed their lives to be controlled and ruined by their acts of bad faith.

More than anyone in *All My Sons*, Joe Keller is guilty of living in bad faith. In the opening stage directions, Miller introduces Keller as follows:

> *Keller is nearing sixty. A heavy man of stolid mind and build, a business man these many years, but with the imprint of the machine-shop worker and boss still upon him. When he reads, when he speaks, when he listens, it is with the terrible concentration of the uneducated man for whom there is still wonder in many commonly known things, a man whose judgments must be dredged out of experience and a peasant-like common sense. A man among men.*

This uneducated businessman with a peasantlike common sense is certainly a man among men in his community. He is respected and admired by just about everyone in his neighborhood, although he has already been convicted of shipping out faulty airplane parts during the Second World War. The exposition informs us that Keller appealed and won his case and firmly stood his ground in the face of public outrage during his trial. But, in spite of his legal victory, some of the neighbors who most admire Keller have never really believed in his innocence and continue to befriend him even though they remain convinced that he has committed a heinous crime. The Keller family has a kind of seductive charm that puts people at ease, and Joe Keller is particularly effective in making the criminal charges against him seem ridiculous. His whole posture to his neighbors seems to be a subtle plea that asks, How could such a swell guy—such a simple and good-natured man—be guilty of those horrible criminal offenses? Of course, in playing the role of the innocent, friendly neighbor, Keller acts in bad faith. As Allen A. Stambusky points out, Keller wears a mask in front of others in an effort not only to convince them of his innocence and good character but also to help him alleviate his guilt:

> Although Keller adopts a "noble" manner of acting after he has committed his crime, he does so out of a sense of guilt, trying somehow to convince himself as well as his neighbors that he is innocent. He goes on living the lie, feigning the "good" fellow, the friendly neighbor, big-hearted and kindly, the "martyr" who can carry well the weight of a false accusation.
>
> ("Arthur Miller: Aristotelian Canons in the Twentieth Century," *Modern American Drama*)

Keller chooses lies and self-deception as a means of temporarily escaping from his guilt and the terrible realization that decisions he made in the past have had devastating consequences. But although he adamantly refuses to admit to himself or anyone else that he has done something wrong, Keller knows in his heart that he is directly responsible for the deaths of twenty-one young pilots who crashed because of faulty machinery his company sold to the army. In fact, Miller suggests as much through Keller's identification with his incarcerated ex-partner and his persistent effort to understand the Deever family's hostility toward their father after his imprisonment. Miller uses this revealing material to convey Keller's guilt and prepare the audience for his eventual confession in act 2 and ultimate admission of guilt in act 3. Miller also seems to suggest that Keller's concern for Deever derives in part not only from knowing that he set up his former partner but also from secretly realizing that his own personal torment has much in common with the alienation Deever experiences.

Keller's guilt is in evidence throughout much of the play. He first seems both "*shamed*" and "*alarmed*" in act 1 when Kate reprimands him for telling children in the neighborhood that he has a jail in his basement. Defensively snapping, "What have I got to hide?" Keller suggests not only that he resents Kate's treatment of him but also that he does, indeed, have something to hide. The jail motif is repeated throughout the play to bring the past into the present and strengthen the association between Keller's crime and his guilt. This motif also demonstrates the reality of the consequences of Keller's actions, and it helps to illustrate the problem with isolating oneself from the outer world. As though he were confined in a jail, Keller views the world as having "a forty-foot front . . . [that] ended at the building line." He alienates himself from others and irresponsibly commits antisocial acts, thinking the whole time that his behavior is excusable because he is only doing what he must to save his business and keep his family comfortable and secure. In other words, Keller believes that anything he does can be justified if whatever he does is for the benefit of his family. He has convinced himself that his sole responsibility in life is to his family, his only obligation in life to be a success so that he can provide for his wife and children. For Keller, "Nothin' is bigger" than the family. Even the setting of the play is designed to reveal and comment on Keller's myopic world view. The entire play takes place in the *"back yard of the Keller home. . . . The stage is hedged on right and left by tall, closely planted poplars which lend the yard a secluded atmosphere."*

As the play progresses, the exposition gradually exposes Keller's secret and simultaneously reveals more about his character. While discussing his trial, Keller boasts of being "exonerated" and then boldly strolling down the street after his release from prison, intentionally suffering the accusing stares of his neighbors while holding "a court paper in [his] pocket to prove" his innocence. As George Deever later tells the Keller family, the court paper proves nothing since Keller won his trial on a technicality: The prosecution could not prove conclusively that Keller gave his ex-partner the order over the telephone to cover up and sell the faulty parts. Therefore, by bragging about his actions on the day of his release from prison, Keller demonstrates not only his lack of remorse but also his inability to see the consequences of his actions. He also incriminates himself by suggesting that he was only innocent because he possessed the court paper, not because he was wrongly accused in the first place.

Keller's guilt is clearly evident when he defends making money at his plant and begs Chris to take his money and use it "without shame . . . with joy." One does not have to listen too closely to Keller to hear what he is really implying in his plea. He knows how he has made his fortune, and he also knows how Chris would respond to the business if he suspected that innocent people died so that his father could make money for his family. Keller knows that George Deever is going to call on them soon, and worries that George and his sister, Ann, will disclose the truth and turn Chris away from him. If Chris can take his money without shame, Keller reasons to himself, then he would have definite assurance of his son's love—and maybe he even deceives himself into believing that with this love will come some kind of silent understanding that will eliminate the need for forgiveness and relieve him of his guilt.

The most overt sign of Keller's guilt in act 1 occurs right before the curtain falls. Concerned about George's impending arrival, Kate warns Keller: "Be smart now, Joe. The boy is coming. Be smart." Keller's theatrically effective response is certainly telling. The previously jovial and gentle Keller storms into the house "*in hopeless fury . . . slamming* [the] *screen door violently behind him.*" Obviously he is as concerned as Kate about the possible disclosure of his criminal offense, and he wants to run away both from Kate's critical look—which reduces him to a pathetic figure—and from the truth. As Marianne Boruch indicates, Keller's sudden transformation at the end of act 1 represents an important stage in his development:

> One imagines the sound of that door haunting the entire intermission. . . . Keller's violence here creates a startling discovery. A man normally talkative, good-natured and friendly has clearly been forced back abruptly, into a dark, confused corner of himself. The slamming of the door not only ends the act; it ends the old Keller we saw moving in act 1. Suddenly, we perceive something new, a deeper tension in the play, as Keller, too, discovers something, a darker creature stirring within.

After a couple of outbursts early in act 2 in which he nearly reveals himself, Keller is finally forced to admit that he made the decision to send out the cracked cylinder heads. Perhaps nowhere in the play is his bad faith more evident than in his stubborn defense of his criminal behavior:

> I'm in business, a man is in business; a hundred and twenty cracked, you're out of business; you got a process, the process don't work you're out of business; you don't know how to operate, your stuff is no good; they close you up, they tear up your contracts, what the hell's it to them? You lay forty years into a business and they knock you out in five minutes, what could I do, let them take forty years, let them take my life away?

According to Keller, his decision is consonant with the American businessman's code of ethics. Evidently, no act is too morally offensive or irresponsible to commit if in doing so he protects his business and keeps it solvent. He justifies his business practices by describing the code of ethics that he saw operating in wartime America:

Who worked for nothin' in that war? When they work for
nothin', I'll work for nothin'. Did they ship a gun or a truck
outa Detroit before they got their price? Is that clean? It's dollars
and cents, nickels and dimes; war and peace, it's nickels and
dimes, what's clean? Half the Goddam country is gotta go if I
go!

In taking this stance, Keller tries to absolve himself from guilt not only by
pretending that he is innocent of any wrongdoing, but also by seeing himself
as the victim of forces beyond his control. Keller refuses to believe that he
was free to act in any other manner than that which he had chosen. He has
convinced himself and seeks to persuade the others that, given the situation
that confronted him, he had only two choices: Either he could take a chance
selling the defective machinery and hope the parts would perform satisfac-
torily or he could let his business fail and watch his family starve. He
believes that he made the best choice possible. Of course, in creating this
either/or dilemma, Keller acts in bad faith. He limits the range of possibilities to only two—one of these is no option at all—and then he deceives
himself into believing that his inability to act freely excuses him from being
held accountable for the fate of the pilots. His antisocial behavior is an act
of bad faith, and then his rationalization in an effort to justify his behavior
merely perpetuates his original project of bad faith.

To understand Joe Keller, however, the audience must not see him as
a man driven by greed. Keller is not a selfish businessman pursuing his
own self-interests and amassing a great fortune for himself; he is an extremely dedicated father and a loving and caring husband. In fact, one could
even say that he is obsessed with his role as provider, and this obsession,
together with his attempt to play the role of the almighty father figure,
also constitutes another major part of his bad faith. Keller sets an impossible
task for himself: He tries to fix his essence by passing himself off as an
almost mythic or godlike presence in his family. In playing the role of the
almighty father, Keller sets himself up for a fall because he can not possibly
live up to the inhuman demands of perfection that such a role requires.
Like Oedipus, Keller lets his pride get the best of him. Keller takes pride
in his role as a father and devotes his life to ensuring that his family is well-
taken-care-of. But, ironically, while trying to preserve this part of his life
that is valuable, Keller actually hastens his own undoing and the destruction
of that which he most prizes. Like Oedipus, Keller unwittingly plunges
headlong into disaster, ensnaring himself in a web of fatal consequences
that originate in his role play. Keller's pride also stems from his insecurity,

particularly from his fear of failure. As Barry Gross perceptively observes, "There is no zealot like a convert and there is probably no more devoted parent than a neglected or an abandoned child"("*All My Sons* and the Larger Context," *Critical Essays on Arthur Miller*, 1979). Keller "was put out . . . [to] earn his keep" when he was only ten years old. As a result, he spends his life trying to compensate for his deprived childhood by working hard to ensure that family problems of the past are not repeated in the present. Ironically, the end result of his labor is that instead of winning the love of those around him he arouses their scorn, and instead of preserving the family he so values he causes its collapse.

The family means so much to Keller because it is the only place where his life has real meaning and significance. In the family, Keller believes he can fix his identity by projecting an image of his own making. He wants to attain a permanent identity by confirming his mental image in the minds of his family members and in doing this achieve a kind of immortality. Like Willy Loman in *Death of a Salesman*, Keller seeks his immortality in the continuity of his son and the preservation of his son's love. Even his business only has meaning in terms of Chris's response to it. If Chris accepts the business, then Keller has succeeded in making his life's work amount to something—something that he can pass on to his son. And if Chris finds value in his business, then perhaps, Keller thinks, he will also love and respect the man who built it and handed it over to him. All that Keller truly cares about is winning the love and approval of his son, for his relationship with Chris is the only proof that his life has meaning. Perhaps even unknowingly, Keller desperately seeks to give his life meaning and dignity through his son's love—and when he thinks he has lost this, he feels that his life ceases to have any purpose. Rather than admit that his life has no meaning, that he has failed as a father and has lost the love and respect of his family, Keller takes refuge in suicide. But in killing himself Keller once again fails to transform guilt into responsibility; he dies as he has lived—in bad faith.

Joe Keller is not the only member of the Keller family to live in bad faith. Kate also resorts to lies and self-deception as a way of contending with the anguish and sorrow she experiences as a result of her son's death in the war. Kate deludes herself into believing that Larry is still alive and will one day magically reappear in their home. She resorts to a blind faith in religion to fortify her conviction, and rationalizes that "God does not let a son be killed by his father." Beyond all reason, she also gives in to a superstitious reliance on astrology, convinced that Larry's horoscope will confirm that he did not die. By pinning all her hopes on the movement of the stars, Kate assures herself that great external forces are at work in the determination of Larry's fate. She acts in bad faith by deluding herself into believing that deterministic forces, not the individual, create one's destiny. She didn't know that Larry deliberately crashed his plane in an absurd protest of his father's criminal activity and in a sincere effort to expiate his father's sins. Interestingly enough when Kate finally learns the truth about Larry's death, she suffers no terrific shock, perhaps secretly believing, although never admitting, that Larry would never return from the war.

Kate also acts in bad faith by lying to herself and to others about her husband's role in the scandal at his shop. Instead of encouraging Keller to face his situation honestly and accept his responsibilities, Kate protects him from persecution by falsely verifying his lie. But her loyalty to her husband only widens the gulf between them. Their awareness of the other's deception makes them uncomfortable together: They experience guilt and shame beneath the accusing looks of each other and know they appear in a degraded object-state in the other's eyes. Kate also acts in bad faith by deciding that Keller is to blame if Larry is dead. Before she learns the truth about Larry's death, she convinces herself that Larry cannot be dead because "God does not let a son be killed by his father." She thinks the only possible way Larry could die is by flying one of the planes with the defective parts manufactured by her husband and refuses to consider any other possibilities. She deludes herself into thinking that if the unmentionable were to happen only one person would bear the blame: her husband. Reaching this conclusion, Kate attempts to ease her conscience by denying her culpability and by fixing her husband's essence in the role of villain. She refuses to believe that he could eventually repudiate his bad faith, and she permanently reduces him to an object of scorn.

Like his mother, Chris Keller also makes his father an object of contempt once he is convinced of his father's guilt. Probably the least likeable character in *All My Sons*, Chris affects a high moral tone and delivers sententious speeches that set him apart from the rest of the characters. As Ronald Hayman observes, too frequently the sentiment in Chris's speeches "is not sufficiently dramatized." But this is not a problem with the play; Miller deliberately uses the discrepancy between Chris's words and actions to develop his character and reveal his bad faith. The idealistic youth who energetically professes to detest "dishonesty" is as guilty as his parents of attempting to hide from reality. Though he persists in pushing his mother toward an acceptance of his brother's death, he does so for selfish motives that have little to do with his mother's ability to deal with reality. And as he indicts his father for irresponsible behavior, he knows that his words sound false because he has suspected his father's guilt all along; but he deliberately avoids confronting the truth—again for purely selfish reasons. In seeing his father's naked humanity, in coming face-to-face with his father's weaknesses, Chris also knows that the truth would force him to see his own imperfections beneath the mask of innocence he wears. Therefore, his father's failure serves as a painful reminder to Chris of his own fallibility.

Chris desperately tries to avoid honest self-appraisal because of his experiences as a company commander in the war. Having watched heroic young men die selflessly in battle to save their comrades, Chris feels guilty for failing these men under his command and surviving the war. His guilt is the guilt of the survivor—the guilt, as Holga tells Quentin in *After the Fall*, that derives from knowing "no one is innocent they did not kill!" Chris wants to escape from the anguish he feels as a result of his survival; so, when given the chance, he tries to find relief by making his father a scapegoat. He casts all his own sins and feelings of guilt onto Keller and hopes that in the destruction of his father his own sins will be expiated. Clearly, Chris's interest in seeing his father brought to justice is at least partially motivated by his own self-interests. He hopes to escape from his anguish and is therefore guilty of acting in bad faith. As Sue Bayliss accurately insinuates, Chris is a hypocrite: "Chris makes people want to be better than it's possible to be. . . . As though Chris or anybody else isn't compromising."

Chris also acts in bad faith by failing to see how his high expectations have contributed to his father's destruction. In a revealing comment, Chris tells Keller why he is so upset by his antisocial behavior: "*I* know you're no worse than most men but I thought you were better. I never saw you as a man. I saw you as my father." Chris, in idolizing his father, has helped to perpetuate his father's bad faith, for it is the son—perhaps even more than the father—who wants to believe in the immutable essence of Keller as a type of almighty father figure. As a result of his self-deception, Chris paves the way for his own disillusionment, thinking his father could be more than a man. Chris acts in bad faith by demanding the impossible: perfection from an imperfect being. Without anticipating the extent of the effect of his expectations on his father, Chris inadvertently reinforces Keller's absurd attempt to impose stasis on his being—and when faced with the unmistakable proof that his image of his father has been just an illusion, Chris still unrealistically expects the kind of noble gesture from Keller that is inconsistent with his father's character. As Benjamin Nelson suggests, both father and son pay heavily for their bad faith: "Each man bears the burden of responsibility—Joe for casting himself in a role he cannot fulfill, and Chris for adamantly maintaining his adolescent adoration of an impossible idol—and each pays for the dichotomy between reality and the illusion he has fostered."

Although they are less fully drawn and not as effectively realized on the stage as the central characters, some of the minor characters in the play also lend dramatic credence to Miller's ideas on bad faith. While the cast could be cut, minor characters like Ann Deever and Jim and Sue Bayliss play significant roles because of the insight they provide into the central characters and the problem of bad faith. Like the Kellers, they withhold the truth from one another to sustain their illusions and protect their happiness. Ann, at the very least, suspects Keller is guilty because of her letter from Larry, but she refrains from disclosing her information until her future happiness with Chris is threatened by Kate's insistence that Larry is not dead. She presents the Kellers with Larry's suicide letter only to protect her own self-interests; her motives are purely selfish, governed by a fundamental drive for self-preservation. Jim and Sue Bayliss also suspect Keller is guilty and refuse to do anything to bring him to justice. In fact, they even seem to admire Keller for pulling "a fast one to get out of jail." Unlike Sue, who envies and resents the Kellers' success, Jim attempts to protect the Kellers from George Deever's hostile accusations and their eventual confrontation with the truth. His interference is interesting because it comments on his own insecurities and feeble effort to escape from reality. He shares their dilemma and tries to shield them, particularly Chris, from the truth because he wants to sustain his illusion of their perfection as long as possible, possibly to preserve his own motivation for wanting "to be better than it's possible to be." Having already watched "The star of [his] honesty . . . go out," Jim knows that he is lost "in the usual darkness." He knows that if he no longer has Chris's image of perfection to inspire him he will find it impossible "to remember the kind of man [he] wanted to be." Therefore, like the Kellers, Jim resorts to bad faith for basically selfish reasons.

One other group of significant minor characters in *All My Sons* includes all the absent figures in the play. One of these, Larry, can hardly be called minor because of the effect he has on the play's action; he is, in essence, the catalyst that propels the action forward. His disappearance is what keeps Kate from accepting Chris's engagement with Ann, while it simultaneously causes Chris to try to convince his mother that Larry is dead so they can get on with their lives. Larry's absence directly leads to Ann's attempt to salvage her life with Chris by disclosing the revealing suicide letter, and it not only convinces Keller—by way of the suicide letter—that he, too, must die but also serves as a comment on his failure to act responsibly toward society. For Larry's death is a protest of his father's crime. However, in electing to die rather than bear the shame of his father's guilt, Larry also acts in bad faith. His death, like the suicide of his father, is essentially an attempt to escape from the shame and humiliation he would inevitably suffer. He dies to escape from his anguish and therefore fails to transform guilt into responsibility. But, unlike Larry, some other absent characters die selflessly and nobly in their valiant effort to save humanity from tyranny and worldwide disaster. They are the nameless soldiers under Chris's command who die in battle during the Second World War. Giving their lives while trying to preserve freedom and life-enhancing values, these anonymous characters provide a model of the kind of responsible behavior that gives meaning and dignity to human existence. Their honorable action is a viable alternative to the bad faith that ruins and, in some cases, even destroys the lives of the other characters.

With his portrayal of Joe Keller's downfall, Miller suggests that every individual has the power to make free choices and the obligation to convert those choices into responsible actions toward society. When one refuses to accept his freedom and denies his responsibility to society, he lives in bad faith. *All My Sons* shows the danger of such bad faith by exploding what Miller calls the "exclusiveness" of private life in America, "the fiction . . . that if every man privately takes care of his own interests, the community and the nation will prosper and be safe" (*Situation Normal*, 1944). Having witnessed the Holocaust, Miller knows better, and in *All My Sons* he destroys that myth and shows why social responsibility is absolutely essential to humanity's survival. The collapse of the Keller family is not just a private affair; it is emblematic of a deeper, broader disintegration of humanistic values that could spell disaster to a world trapped in its own bad faith.

# Chronology

1915    Born October 17 in New York City, second son of Isadore and Augusta Miller.

1929    Depression causes financial difficulties in father's clothing business. Family moves to Brooklyn.

1934    Enters the University of Michigan, Ann Arbor. Studies journalism.

1936    First play, *Honors at Dawn,* produced. Wins Hopwood Awards in Drama for *No Villain* (1936) and *Honors at Dawn* (1937), and Theatre Guild Bureau of New Plays Award for *They Too Arise.*

1938    Receives Bachelor of Arts from University of Michigan. Begins work with the Federal Theatre Project.

1940    Marries Mary Grace Slattery.

1944    Visits army camps collecting material for screenplay, *The Story of G.I. Joe. Situation Normal* (prose account of this tour) published. *The Man Who Had All the Luck* published and produced in New York; wins Theatre Guild National Prize.

1945    Novel, *Focus,* published.

1947    *All My Sons* produced and published in New York; wins New York Drama Critics' Circle Award.

1949    *Death of a Salesman* published and produced; wins Pulitzer Prize and New York Drama Critics' Circle Award.

1950    Adaptation of Ibsen's *An Enemy of the People* produced.

1953    *The Crucible* produced and published.

1954    Is refused passport by State Department to attend opening of *The Crucible* in Brussels.

1955    *A Memory of Two Mondays* and the one-act version of *A View from the Bridge* produced and published in New York.

1956    Two-act version of *A View from the Bridge* produced in London. Divorces Mary Slattery. Appears before House Un-American Activities Committee. Marries Marilyn Monroe.

1957    Convicted of contempt of Congress for refusing to name sus-
        pected communists. *Collected Plays* published.

1958    Conviction reversed by Supreme Court. Elected to the National
        Arts and Letters Institute.

1960    Filming of *The Misfits*. Separates from Marilyn Monroe.

1961    *The Misfits* released. Divorces Marilyn Monroe. *The Misfits* pub-
        lished as a novel.

1962    Marries Austrian-born photographer Ingeborg Morath. Birth of
        daughter Rebecca Augusta Miller.

1964    *After the Fall* and *Incident at Vichy* produced by the Lincoln Center
        Repertory Theatre.

1965    Elected International President of PEN (Poets, Essayists, and
        Novelists).

1967    *I Don't Need You Anymore,* a collection of short stories, published.

1968    *The Price* published and produced in New York. Serves as delegate
        to Democratic National Convention.

1969    *In Russia* published with Inge Morath.

1970    *Fame* produced in New York.

1972    *The Creation of the World and Other Business* produced in New
        York. Serves as delegate to the Democratic National Convention.

1974    *Up from Paradise* (musical version of *The Creation of the World*)
        produced in Ann Arbor, Michigan.

1977    *The Archbishop's Ceiling* produced at the Kennedy Center in Wash-
        ington, D.C. *In the Country* published with Inge Morath.

1978    Visits China with Inge Morath. *The Theater Essays of Arthur Miller*
        published.

1980    *The American Clock* produced in New York. *Playing for Time,*
        television adaptation of Fania Fenelon's book, wins an Emmy.

1982    Two one-acts, *Some Kind of Love Story* and *Elegy for a Lady,* open
        at the Long Wharf Theater in New Haven.

1983    Directs *Death of a Salesman* in China with Chinese cast.

1984    Revival of *Death of a Salesman* opens on Broadway with Dustin
        Hoffman as Willy Loman.

1985    Telecast of 1984 production of *Death of a Salesman*.

# Contributors

HAROLD BLOOM, Sterling Professor of the Humanities at Yale University, is the author of *The Anxiety of Influence, Poetry and Repression,* and many other volumes of literary criticism. His forthcoming study, *Freud: Transference and Authority,* attempts a full-scale reading of all of Freud's major writings. A MacArthur Prize Fellow, he is general editor of five series of literary criticism published by Chelsea House. During 1987–88, he served as Charles Eliot Norton Professor of Poetry at Harvard University.

HAROLD CLURMAN, the distinguished director and critic, is the author of *The Fervent Years: The Group Theatre and the Thirties* and *On Directing,* among other books.

SAMUEL A. YORKS has taught English at Portland State College.

ARVIN R. WELLS is Professor of English at Ohio University. He is the author of *Jesting Moses: A Study in Cabellian Comedy.*

SHEILA HUFTEL is the author of *Arthur Miller: The Burning Glass.*

EDWARD MURRAY is Professor of English at the State University of New York, Brockport. His books include *Arthur Miller: Dramatist* and *Fellini the Artist.*

BARRY GROSS is Professor of English at Michigan State University, East Lansing. He has written extensively on F. Scott Fitzgerald.

ORM ÖVERLAND is Professor of American Literature at the University of Bergen, Norway. He is the author of *The Making and Meaning of an American Classic: James Fenimore Cooper's "The Prairie"* and *America Perceived: A View from Abroad in the Twentieth Century.*

DENNIS WELLAND is Professor of American Literature at the University of Manchester. He founded and for ten years edited the *Journal of American*

*Studies* and is the author of *Mark Twain and England* and *Wilfred Owen: A Critical Study*.

LEONARD MOSS is Professor of Comparative Literature at the State University of New York, Geneseo. In addition to his full-length study of Arthur Miller, he has written on Aeschylus, Seneca, Milton, and Kafka.

C. W. E. BIGSBY is Senior Lecturer in American Literature at the University of East Anglia. His books include *David Mamet, Confrontation and Commitment, Dada and Surrealism, Superculture: American Popular Culture and Europe,* and the three-volume *Critical Introduction to Twentieth-Century American Drama*.

JUNE SCHLUETER is Associate Professor of English at Lafayette College. Her books include *Metafictional Characters in Modern Drama* and *The Plays and Drama of Peter Handke*.

STEVEN R. CENTOLA is Assistant Professor of English at Millersville University, Pennsylvania, and is completing a book-length study of Miller's plays.

# Bibliography

Bentley, Eric. "Back to Broadway." *Theatre Arts* 33 (November 1949): 10–19.
————."On the Waterfront." In *What Is Theatre?* New York: Beacon, 1956: 98–102, 222–25.
Bermel, Albert. "Right, Wrong and Mr. Miller." *New York Times,* 14 April 1968.
Bigsby, C. W. E. "Arthur Miller." In *Confrontation and Commitment: A Study of Contemporary American Drama.* Columbia: University of Missouri Press, 1967.
Blumberg, Paul. "Sociology and Social Literature: Work Alienation in the Plays of Arthur Miller." *American Quarterly* 21 (1969): 291–310.
Boruch, Marianne. "Miller and Things." *Literary Review* 24, no. 4 (Summer 1981): 548–61.
Brashear, William R. "The Empty Bench: Morality, Tragedy, and Arthur Miller." *Michigan Quarterly Review* 5 (1966): 270–78.
Brater, Enoch. "Ethics and Ethnicity in the Plays of Arthur Miller." In *From Hester Street to Hollywood: The Jewish-American Stage and Screen,* edited by Sarah Blacker Cohen. Bloomington: Indiana University Press, 1983.
Bronson, David. "*An Enemy of the People:* A Key to Arthur Miller's Art and Ethics." *Comparative Drama* 2 (1968): 229–47.
Broussard, Louis. *American Drama: Contemporary Allegory from Eugene O'Neill to Tennessee Williams,* 116–21. Norman: University of Oklahoma Press, 1962.
Brustein, Robert. "Arthur Miller's Mea Culpa." *The New Republic* 150 (8 February 1964): 26–30.
Centola, Steven R. "Confrontation with the Other: Alienation in the Works of Arthur Miller and Jean-Paul Sartre." *Journal of Evolutionary Psychology* 1–2 (March 1984): 1–11.
Coen, Frank. "Teaching the Drama." *English Journal* 56 (1967): 1136–39.
Cohn, Ruby. "The Articulate Victims of Arthur Miller." In *Dialogue in American Drama, 68–96.* Bloomington: Indiana University Press, 1971.
Collins, Anthony R. "Arthur Miller and the Judgement of God." *South Central Bulletin* 42 (1982): 120–24.
Corrigan, Robert W., ed. *Arthur Miller: A Collection of Critical Essays.* Englewood Cliffs, N.J.: Prentice-Hall, 1969.
Dworkin, Martin. "Miller and Ibsen." *Humanist* 11 (1951): 110–15.
Flaxman, Seymour L. "The Debt of Williams and Miller to Ibsen and Strindberg." *Comparative Literature Studies,* Special Advance Issue (1963): 51–59.

Foulkes, A. P. *Literature and Propaganda*. London: Methuen, 1983.

Freedman, Morris. "Bertolt Brecht and American Social Drama." In *The Moral Impulse: Modern Drama from Ibsen to the Present*, 99–114. Carbondale: Southern Illinois University Press, 1967.

Ganz, Arthur. "The Silence of Arthur Miller." *Drama Survey* 3 (1963): 224–37.

Gassner, John. *Form and Idea in Modern Theatre*, 109–49. New York: Dryden, 1956.

Gollub, Christian-Albrecht. "Interview with Arthur Miller." *Michigan Quarterly Review* 16 (1977): 121–41.

Hayashi, Tetsumaro. *An Index to Arthur Miller Criticism*. Metuchen, N.J.: Scarecrow, 1976.

Hayman, Ronald. *Arthur Miller*. London: Heinemann, 1970.

———. "Arthur Miller: Between Sartre and Society." *Encounter* 37 (1971): 73–79.

Hays, Peter L. "Arthur Miller and Tennessee Williams." *Essays in Literature* 4 (1977): 239–49.

Heilman, Robert Bechtold. "Arthur Miller." In *The Iceman, the Arsonist, and the Troubled Agent: Tragedy and Melodrama on the Modern Stage*, 142–64. Seattle: University of Washington Press, 1973.

Hynes, Joseph A. "Arthur Miller and the Impasse of Naturalism." *South Atlantic Quarterly* 62 (1963): 327–34.

Inserillo, Charles R. "Wish and Desire: Two Poles of the Imagination in the Drama of Arthur Miller and T. S. Eliot." *Xavier University Studies* 1 (1962): 247–58.

Loughlin, Richard L. "Tradition and Tragedy in *All My Sons*." *English Record* 14 (1964): 23–27.

Martin, Robert A., ed. *Arthur Miller: New Perspectives*. Englewood Cliffs, N.J.: Prentice-Hall, 1982.

McMahon, Helen. "Arthur Miller's Common Man: The Problem of the Realistic and the Mythic." *Drama and Theatre* 10 (1972): 128–33.

Miles, O. Thomas. "Three Authors in Search of a Character." *Personalist* 46 (1965): 65–72.

Miller, Jeanne-Marie A. "Odets, Miller, and Communism." *College Language Association Journal* 19 (1976): 484–93.

Morehouse, Ward. "Arthur Miller." In *Matinee Tomorrow: 50 Years of Our Theatre*, by Ward Morehouse, pp. 290–91. New York: Whittlesey House, 1949.

Nelson, Benjamin. *Arthur Miller*. London: Owen, 1970.

Popkin, Henry. "Arthur Miller: The Strange Encounter." *Sewanee Review* 68 (1960): 34–60.

———. "Arthur Miller Out West." *Commentary* 31 (1961): 433–36.

Prudhoe, John. "Arthur Miller and the Tradition of Tragedy." *English Studies* 43 (1962): 430–39.

Rajuhishnan, V. "After Commitment: An Interview with Arthur Miller." *Theatre Journal* 32, no. 2 (1980): 196–204.

Tynan, Kenneth. *Curtains*. New York: Atheneum, 1961.

Vogel, Dan. "Willy Tyrannos." In *The Three Masks of American Tragedy*, 91–102. Baton Rouge: Louisiana State University Press, 1974.

Wells, Arvin R. "The Living and the Dead in *All My Sons*." *Modern Drama* 7 (1964): 46–51.

# Acknowledgments

"The Question of Relatedness" (originally entitled "Introduction") by Arthur Miller from *Arthur Miller's Collected Plays* by Arthur Miller. Reprinted by permission of International Creative Management, Inc. © 1957 by Arthur Miller.

"Thesis and Drama" (originally entitled "Arthur Miller: 1947") by Harold Clurman from *Lies Like Truth: Theatre Reviews and Essays* by Harold Clurman, © 1947, 1958, and renewed 1975 by Harold Clurman; © renewed 1986 by Juleen Compton. Reprinted by permission of Macmillan Publishing Company.

"Joe Keller and His Sons" by Samuel A. Yorks from *Western Humanities Review* 13, no. 4 (Autumn 1959), © 1959 by the University of Utah. Reprinted by permission.

"The Living and the Dead in *All My Sons*" by Arvin R. Wells from *Modern Drama* 7, no. 1 (May 1964), © 1964 by the University of Toronto, Graduate Centre for the Study of Drama. Reprinted by permission of *Modern Drama*.

"Miller, Ibsen, and Organic Drama" (originally entitled "*All My Sons*") by Sheila Huftel from *Arthur Miller: The Burning Glass* by Sheila Huftel, © 1965 by Sheila Huftel. Reprinted by permission of Lyle Stuart, Inc.

"The Failure of Social Vision" (originally entitled "*All My Sons*") by Edward Murray from *Arthur Miller, Dramatist* by Edward Murray, © 1967 by Frederick Ungar Publishing Co., Inc. Reprinted by permission of Crossroad/Ungar/Continuum.

"*All My Sons* and the Larger Context" by Barry Gross from *Modern Drama* 18, no. 1 (March 1975), © 1975 by the University of Toronto, Graduate Centre for the Study of Drama. Reprinted by permission of *Modern Drama*.

"The Action and Its Significance: Miller's Struggle with Dramatic Form" (originally entitled "The Action and Its Significance: Arthur Miller's Struggle with Dramatic Form") by Orm Överland from *Modern Drama* 18, no. 1 (March 1975), © 1975 by the University of Toronto, Graduate Centre for the Study of Drama. Reprinted by permission of *Modern Drama*.

141

"Two Early Plays" (originally entitled "Three Early Plays") by Dennis Welland from *Miller: A Study of His Plays* by Dennis Welland, © 1979 by Dennis Welland. Reprinted by permission of Methuen & Co. Ltd., London.

"*All My Sons*" by Leonard Moss from *Arthur Miller* by Leonard Moss, © 1980 by G. K. Hall & Co., Inc., Boston. Reprinted by permission. All rights reserved.

"Realism and Idealism" (originally entitled "Drama from a Living Center") by C. W. E. Bigsby from *A Critical Introduction to Twentieth-Century American Drama 2: Tennessee Williams, Arthur Miller, Edward Albee* by C. W. E. Bigsby, © 1984 by C. W. E. Bigsby. Reprinted by permission of the author and Cambridge University Press.

"The Dramatic Strategy of *All My Sons*" by June Schlueter from *Arthur Miller,* edited by June Schlueter and James K. Flanagan, © 1987 by Crossroad/Ungar/Continuum. Reprinted by permission of Crossroad/Ungar/Continuum.

"Bad Faith and *All My Sons*" by Steven R. Centola, © 1988 by Steven R. Centola. Published for the first time in this volume. Printed by permission.

# Index